Foucault's Law

Foucault's Law is the first book in almost fifteen years to address the question of Foucault's position on law. Readings of Foucault's conception of law usually start from the proposition that he failed to consider the role of law in modernity, or indeed that he deliberately marginalized it. In canvassing a wealth of primary and secondary sources, the authors of *Foucault's Law* rebut this argument. They argue that, far from marginalizing law, Foucault develops a much more radical, nuanced and coherent theory of law than his various critics have acknowledged. For Golder and Fitzpatrick, Foucault's law is not the contained creature of conventional accounts but is, rather, uncontainable and illimitable. In their radical re-reading, they show how Foucault outlines a concept of law which is not tied to any given form or subordinated to a particular source of power, but is in fact critically oriented towards alterity, towards new possibilities and different ways of being.

Foucault's Law is an important and original contribution to the debate on Foucault and law. The book engages not only with Foucault's diverse writings on law and legal theory but also with the extensive interpretive literature on the topic. Developing as it does a revelatory argument about one of the most important social theorists and philosophers of the twentieth century, the book should be of interest to students and scholars working in the fields of law and social theory, legal theory, and law and philosophy of law, as well as to students of Foucault's work generally.

Ben Golder is a lecturer in law at the University of New South Wales, Australia.

Peter Fitzpatrick is Anniversary Professor of Law at Birkbeck, University of London.

Foucault's Law

Ben Golder and Peter Fitzpatrick

Routledge
Taylor & Francis Group

a GlassHouse book

First published 2009 by Routledge
2 Park Square, Milton Park, Abingdon, Oxon, OX14 4RN

Simultaneously published in the USA and Canada
by Routledge
270 Madison Avenue, New York, NY 10016

Routledge is an imprint of the Taylor & Francis Group, an informa business

A GlassHouse book

© 2009 Ben Golder and Peter Fitzpatrick

Typeset in Sabon by Taylor & Francis Books
Printed and bound in Great Britain by CPI Rowe, Chippenham, Wiltshire

British Library Cataloguing in Publication Data
A catalogue record for this book is available from the British Library

Library of Congress Cataloging in Publication Data
Golder, Ben.
 Foucault's law / Ben Golder and Peter Fitzpatrick.
  p. cm.
 1. Law–Philosophy. 2. Foucault, Michel, 1926–1984. 3. Sociological jurisprudence. I.
Fitzpatrick, Peter, 1941– II. Title.
 K230.F682G65 2009
 340′.1–dc22
                    2008040545

ISBN10: 0-415-42453-4 (hbk)
ISBN13: 978-0-415-42453-0 (hbk)

ISBN10: 0-415-42454-2 (pbk)
ISBN13: 978-0-415-42454-7 (pbk)

ISBN10: 0-203-88056-0 (ebk)
ISBN13: 978-0-203-88056-2 (ebk)

To Emily

Contents

Acknowledgements

Several people and groups have been influential in shaping our ideas and providing critical perspectives on previous versions of chapters. We thank all the staff and students of the School of Law, Birkbeck who have shared discussions with us, and in particular members of the PhD Discussion Group on Law and Social Theory. Specific parts of the book were presented as papers at the 2007 Critical Legal Conference and at a Staff Workshop on 'The Laws of Michel Foucault' in 2008 (both held at Birkbeck). We thank participants on both these occasions for their critiques and contributions, but particular thanks are due to Lissa Lincoln, Véronique Voruz and Andrew Sharpe for their engagement and dialogue. In the final stages of writing, the Law Theory Group at the University of Warwick also provided generative insights on specific chapters of the book. At Routledge, we have benefited greatly from the creative editorial work of Colin Perrin and the timely production assistance of Holly Davis. They have been an excellent team with which to work. For exemplary indexing we thank Chris Lloyd, for proofreading and editorial guidance we thank John Golder, and for an abundance of references and insight we thank Pablo Sanges Ghetti.

Beginnings

... we are always in the position of beginning again.[1]

Ironically, in the years since Jean Baudrillard's polemic exhortation to 'forget Foucault'[2] the number of titles devoted to Foucault and his work has risen enormously.[3] In the face of such an ascendance, fulfilling Baudrillard's injunction is today becoming all the more difficult. And as this task of forgetting becomes progressively more difficult, the fecundity of the rememberings increases also. As the titles of recent productions on Foucault aptly attest (we are thinking, for example, of Jeffrey T. Nealon's *Foucault Beyond Foucault: Power and Its Intensifications Since 1984* and Eric Paras's *Foucault 2.0: Beyond Power and Knowledge*), the discursive contest over the (re)positioning and (re)imagining of the Foucaultian legacy proceeds with unabated alacrity.[4] Why, then, another recollective book on Foucault?

Our contribution to the (re)imagining of Foucault takes place in a field (law and legal theory) which up until now has received much less attention than other disciplines such as history, philosophy, political theory and criminology. To date, a fully elaborated Foucaultian jurisprudence still eludes us. Despite the evident purchase that Foucault's work has enjoyed in cognate fields in the arts, humanities and social sciences, his influence in theoretical studies of law has not been felt as keenly. Indeed, in the only monograph to date which takes Foucault's engagement with law as its major point of departure, the authors Alan Hunt and Gary Wickham observe that, '[o]ne of the stimuli for this exploration of Foucault on law is the serious lack of attention his work has attracted from those who make law the central focus of their work'.[5] Hunt and Wickham propose two reasons as to why, at least in 1994 when their *Foucault and Law* was published, this might have been the case: first, the relative inattention to law within Foucault's own work; and, second, the 'long-standing intellectual insularity' of the dominant Anglo-American jurisprudential tradition.[6] Whether or not Hunt and Wickham's second diagnosis of intellectual insularity within analytical and positivist jurisprudence is accurate – and the indictment is hardly a novel, or indeed a particularly contentious, one – it is the first diagnosis with which we are primarily concerned in this book. As Hunt and Wickham go on to argue at some length in *Foucault and Law*, Foucault's relative inattention to law is in fact not simply an inattention on his part but rather an active exclusion of, or failure to properly theorize, the law. In their view, a view with which we engage more extensively in the first chapter, Foucault marginalizes and 'expels' law from modernity. For Hunt and Wickham, and for many scholars in law who have taken their interpretation of Foucault as a point of reference, Foucault (most evidently in books such as *Discipline and Punish* and the first volume of *The History of Sexuality*) narrates the demise of law. In Foucault's modernity, law has been overtaken by the more insinuative and productive powers of discipline or bio-power.[7]

Our book proposes a reading of Foucault's stance on law radically different from the now orthodox understanding that Foucault relegated law to a position of inferiority or irrelevance in modernity. With Hunt and Wickham (and numerous others), we agree that Foucault's law is indeed often made the instrument and accessory of powers external to it. Foucault gives ample evidence in his writings of the mid-1970s of how disciplinary and bio-political operatives and knowledges come to invade and inscribe themselves within modern law, and of how law is co-opted by disciplinary and bio-political imperatives. However, where we depart from Hunt and Wickham's thesis is in our perceiving something radically uncontainable in Foucault's law. In our reading, whilst we agree that Foucault does instrumentally reduce law (and in this sense it is understandable that his critics point to law being contained and thus surpassed in his account of modernity), this reduction is not, and never can be, total. Law in Foucault's account can never be entirely contained and subsumed. Indeed, the 'essence' of Foucault's law (if there is such a thing) is in its very non-essence, its very uncontainability and illimitability. Our argument is that in his work Foucault sketches two different dimensions of law: law as a determinate and contained entity, and law as thoroughly illimitable and as responsive to what lies outside or beyond its position for the time being. Foucault's law, we shall see, is 'located' in the uneasy, ambivalent relation of these two opposed yet generatively interacting legal dimensions. It is in the movement between these two apparently opposed dimensions that Foucault's law is revealed as a law of possibility, contingency and lability: that is, as a law always open to the possibility of its being otherwise. What we seek to do is to return to Foucault's law that sense of constitutive instability (and hence, for us, *promise*) that characterizes his mid-career reflections on power as relational and his later reconceptualization of ethics as an ongoing, constituent project of self-formation. In the chapters that follow this one we shall obviously refine and develop this perspective through a discussion not only of Foucault's own statements on law but also of the diverse interpretations of Foucault's position on law given by legal theorists and other commentators. In Chapter 1, we commence by discussing Hunt and Wickham's contention that Foucault expelled law from modernity (the 'expulsion thesis') at greater length, before addressing several different re-readings of Foucault's position on law. In Chapter 2, we aim to build upon these different readings in order to develop our own interpretation of Foucault's law. As we have just observed, our interpretation of Foucault's law departs from previous ones not simply in our arguing that Foucault does not marginalize or expel law from modernity but, rather more pointedly, in our discerning a certain impelling dynamic to law in Foucault's account. That dynamic, that formative movement of Foucault's law, reveals how law is a constant movement between determinacy and an illimitable responsiveness to alterity. Finally, in Chapter 3, we show how this particular quality of law in fact demonstrates that law – in Foucault's understanding – is a constituent source of our being-together in and as society.

However, before we engage with the contending interpretations of Foucault's position on law in Chapter 1, we need to make two preliminary clarifications and refinements of perspective concerning the existing scholarship on 'Foucault and law' (and the place of our contribution within that scholarship). Our first clarification is in fact a word of caution which may appear somewhat incongruous, or question-begging, coming from the authors of a book entitled *Foucault's Law* (but which will come as little surprise to more seasoned readers of Foucault). Our warning is simply that there is no such thing as Foucault's theory of law, if our expectations of a 'theory' about law are that it provides a circumscribed explanation of its object that is universally valid in all circumstances. For a thinker who conceives of his theoretical project as, at least in part, a challenge to the 'inhibiting effect specific to totalitarian theories',[8] it would perhaps be surprising if we were to find within his work a self-contained, systematic and ordered theory of law. Indeed, it would on these grounds be surprising to find a theory of *anything* in Foucault – rather, he was insistent on numerous occasions that what he was developing was 'neither a theory nor a methodology';[9] not a general explanatory theory of modernity but rather a situated 'analytics' of the operation of power in diverse social practices.[10] Not only did Foucault repeatedly disclaim any attempt to 'theorize' in some grand, universal sense of the word 'theory', but he was also famously resistant to requests to systematize his thought. The imagined dialogue in the 'Introduction' to *The Archaeology of Knowledge*, with an interlocutor who questions Foucault about the trajectory of his work, is perhaps the best-known example of this tendency. At one stage in the passage Foucault remarks:

> Do not ask who I am and do not ask me to remain the same: leave it to our bureaucrats and our police to see that our papers are in order. At least spare us their morality when we write.[11]

This (supposed anti-)theoretical stance, allied to Foucault's somewhat fragmentary reflections on law, has understandably caused some little consternation amongst legal theorists seeking a circumscribed and universally applicable Foucaultian theory of law, or at least searching within his work for a coherent study devoted in whole or in large part to the law. For example, we frequently encounter within 'legal' studies of Foucault the lament that Foucault 'never seriously investigated legal matters',[12] that 'his concern with law was largely incidental to ... [his critical] enterprise'[13] and that, perhaps as a result, he 'had little directly to say about law'.[14] On one level there is some merit in these criticisms. It is true that despite Foucault's persistent interest in legal processes (we might recall his publication of the dossier on the case of Pierre Rivière and his fascination with medico-legal and legal psychiatric evidence in the lecture course *Abnormal*),[15] he never wrote a book-length study of legal forms in the way he did of the prison, the mental asylum, or apparatuses of sexuality. However, as this book will we hope demonstrate, there is indeed much in Foucault which bears directly on law and is of pointed relevance to a theoretical understanding of modern law. Even in those texts where Foucault is traditionally understood as having relegated the law to a position of inferiority and instrumental subordination to the emergent forms of power in modernity, there is a much richer consideration of law than he is usually given credit for by his detractors. We simply want to observe at this point that what we find within Foucault's dispersed comments on law is assuredly nothing like a 'theory' of law as it has conventionally been understood in certain traditions of legal theory – there is no claim, for example, to encapsulate or reduce law to either rule or principle in Foucault's work. On this question of whether Foucault provides a 'theory', however, we do not have to subscribe to the notion of theory as some kind of comprehensively contained coherence in order to read and use Foucault's work as such. Neither does it follow that simply because Foucault on occasions refused the role of theorist, we cannot think and write about his work in these terms. Our position is that Foucault's self-professed objection to theory is somewhat overstated and that once we realize that Foucault was simply expressing an epistemological aversion to a certain type of universal, rational and putatively comprehensive theory, and once we put aside such preconceptions about theory, then we can appreciate that Foucault does indeed theorize law.

The second of our two clarifications mentioned earlier is to draw a distinction between two approaches to Foucault in contemporary legal scholarship. We do this in order to situate our own approach in this book. The first approach, which we might broadly call 'exegetical', or 'interpretive', is the one which we have been discussing. It attempts to locate the position of law within Foucault's existing (and indeed post-humously expanding) body of work. It seeks to answer such questions as: how Foucault conceived of the law; what importance he assigned to it within his overall philosophical framework; and how it relates to his successive formulations of disciplinary power, bio-power, governmentality, and so forth. The second approach, which we might call 'applied', or 'appropriative', seeks to employ Foucaultian concepts and methodologies in the critical study of law.[16] Scholarship in this vein has proceeded relatively unencumbered by the exegetical debates around whether, and to what extent, Foucault theorized law. Legal critics in this field have applied Foucaultian concepts and methodologies such as 'power/knowledge' or genealogy to a range of different legal doctrines, phenomena and contexts without first feeling the need to synthesize Foucault's disparate statements on law or to explicitly (re)construct his overall position on law as a precondition to using his work. In so doing, they have developed a piecemeal Foucaultian jurisprudence which addresses a wide range of legal topics, such as: workplace relations;[17] administrative law;[18] constitutional law;[19] international human rights law;[20] and legal education.[21] Such an approach is entirely consonant with Foucault's oft-repeated methodological pronouncements on how he wished his work to be used – that is, as a 'toolkit' for activists, scholars and writers engaged in a specific field[22] – even if, in places, the limited and tactical employment of some of Foucault's concepts occasions a certain conceptual violence to his broader arguments and critical focus.[23] However, for all the inventiveness and utility of these varied approaches, it is nevertheless the first, exegetical, strain of Foucaultian legal scholarship with which we are concerned. What we are trying to do in this book is to reverse standard understandings of the place and function of law within Foucault's thought.

Finally, in an introductory chapter it is appropriate not just that we attempt to orient the reader but that we also reveal something of our own theoretical orientation in approaching Foucault in the way in which we do in this book. The reading of Foucault's law which we construct in this book is, broadly speaking, a poststructuralist one. Our reading is impelled in large measure by the theorization of law provided by Jacques Derrida,[24] and especially in the latter part of Chapter 2 and throughout Chapter 3 we read Foucault from a poststructuralist perspective. Most legal scholarship on Foucault and Derrida emphasizes the divergences in theoretical approaches between the two thinkers,[25] and Foucault would not invariably have seen his project in the theoretical terms we employ here,[26] but the trend of our argument in this book (especially in Chapters 2 and 3) is to demonstrate certain affinities between the two thinkers on the topic of law. In this endeavour our re-reading of Foucault is perhaps at its most Foucaultian, for in seeking to retrieve, re-read and extend Foucault's thoughts on law we place ourselves within his critical legacy, the legacy of *penser autrement*, of thinking law (and indeed Foucault himself) otherwise. As a first step towards this goal, we now turn to engage with the argument that Foucault expelled law from his analyses of modern society.

Notes

1 Michel Foucault, 'What is Enlightenment?', in *Essential Works of Foucault 1954–1984, Vol. 1: Ethics, Subjectivity and Truth*, trans. Robert Hurley *et al.*, ed. Paul Rabinow (Harmondsworth: Allen Lane/Penguin, 1997), pp. 303–19 (p. 317).

2 Jean Baudrillard, *Forget Foucault*, trans. Nicole Dufresne (Los Angeles: Semiotext(e), 2007).

3 And it continues, even after Foucault's death: 'Although he's been dead for more than two decades, Michel Foucault's work has decisively lived on in academia – even after the so-called death of theory. In humanities and social sciences scholarship, Foucault's work has been and remains by far the most cited of the "big names" associated with theory. In 2005, for example, the Arts and Humanities and Social Sciences Citation Index turns up 1,535 hits for Michel Foucault, 1,016 for Jacques Derrida, 590 for Gilles Deleuze, and 403 for Jacques Lacan. These numbers have grown more or less consistently for the past several years: since the late 1990s, Foucault has generally led the way every year with around 1,000 citations.' Jeffrey T. Nealon, *Foucault Beyond Foucault: Power and Its Intensifications Since 1984* (Stanford, CA: Stanford University Press, 2008), p. 1.

4 Eric Paras, *Foucault 2.0: Beyond Power and Knowledge* (New York: Other Press, 2006).

5 Alan Hunt and Gary Wickham, *Foucault and Law: Towards a Sociology of Law as Governance* (London: Pluto Press, 1994), p. vii. In terms of mono-graphic treatment of the topic, see also Vikki Bell, *Interrogating Incest: Feminism, Foucault and the Law* (London: Routledge, 1993), which engages

issues of Foucault and law from the perspective of a particular question: that of the feminist discourse surrounding incest.

6 Hunt and Wickham, *Foucault and Law*, p. vii. From a certain vantage point the two contentions are of course intimately related. In a question that is itself revealing of the besetting solipsism of much Anglo-American jurisprudential thought, Hugh Baxter asks: 'If Foucault's work offers no plausible account of law, why should legal scholars take him seriously?' See Hugh Baxter, 'Bringing Foucault into Law and Law into Foucault' (1996) 48 (2) *Stanford Law Review* 449, 450. For a similar questioning of Foucault, this time from the discipline of geography, see the interview: Michel Foucault, 'Questions on Geography', in *Power/Knowledge: Selected Interviews and Other Writings 1972–1977*, trans. Colin Gordon et al., ed. Colin Gordon (Brighton: Harvester Press, 1980), pp. 63–77 (pp. 65–67).

7 A related charge, which often attends (or informs) the interpretation of Foucault just instanced, is that Foucault did not just perceive the demise of law but positively welcomed it. According to Petra Gehring, for example, Foucault (along with Nietzsche and Benjamin) was one of the 'radical thinkers of the *limits* of order who ... never made peace with the *legal order* ... [and who in] saying no to law ... defended [his] way of thinking the extreme' (see Petra Gehring, 'Can the Legal Order "Respond"?' (2006) 13 *Ethical Perspectives* 469, 489 (emphasis in original)). Whilst in certain places Foucault strenuously rejects a certain form of law, or legal order (we are thinking, for example, of his comments in Michel Foucault, 'On Popular Justice: A Discussion with Maoists', in *Power/Knowledge*, pp. 1–36), Gehring – and many legal theorists who implicitly assume what she states here – is too quick to locate Foucault's radicalism in a desire to go beyond or do away with law. *Contra* this reading, and echoing Gehring's title, we argue that Foucault's radicalism consists in his discerning an ethos of responsiveness to alterity and going beyond determinate limits as a necessary dimension of law.

8 Michel Foucault, *'Society Must Be Defended': Lectures at the Collège de France, 1975–76*, trans. David Macey (London: Allen Lane, 2003), p. 6. Note that the first two lectures of this course were initially published in English as Michel Foucault, 'Two Lectures', in *Power/Knowledge*, pp. 78–108. We refer throughout to the more recent translation of these lectures in *'Society Must Be Defended'*. On the topic of theory and the role of the theoretician, see 'Intellectuals and Power: A Conversation between Michel Foucault and Gilles Deleuze', in *Language, Counter-Memory, Practice: Selected Essays and Interviews*, trans. Donald F. Bouchard and Sherry Simon, ed. Donald F. Bouchard (Ithaca, NY: Cornell University Press, 1977), pp. 205–17. Of course, that Foucault conceived his critical project in these terms should not blind the reader to the fact that, on many occasions, he was by no means averse to making meta-historical or theoretical generalizations of a quite remarkable scope. There is a revealing tension in his work between this denial of theory and the making of quite extravagant theoretical claims.

9 Michel Foucault, 'The Subject and Power', in *Essential Works of Foucault 1954–1984, Vol. 3: Power*, trans. Robert Hurley et al., ed. James D. Faubion (New York: New Press, 2000), pp. 326–48 (p. 326). See also his comment that: 'I am not developing a theory of power' (Michel Foucault, 'Critical Theory/Intellectual History', in *Politics, Philosophy, Culture: Interviews*

and Other Writings, 1977–1984, trans. Alan Sheridan *et al.*, ed. Lawrence D. Kritzman (London: Routledge, 1988), pp. 17–46 (p. 39)).

10 Michel Foucault, *The Will to Knowledge: The History of Sexuality*, Vol. 1, trans. Robert Hurley (Harmondsworth: Penguin, 1979), p. 82.

11 Michel Foucault, *The Archaeology of Knowledge*, trans. A. M. Sheridan Smith (London: Routledge, 1972), p. 17. See also: 'As to those for whom to work hard, to begin and begin again, to attempt and be mistaken, to go back and rework everything from top to bottom, and still find reason to hesitate from one step to the next – as to those, in short, for whom to work in the midst of uncertainty and apprehension is tantamount to failure, all I can say is that clearly we are not from the same planet' (Michel Foucault, *The Use of Pleasure: The History of Sexuality*, Vol. 2, trans. Robert Hurley (Harmondsworth: Penguin, 1992), p. 7).

12 Baxter, 'Bringing Foucault into Law and Law into Foucault', p. 464.

13 Carole Smith, 'The Sovereign State v Foucault: Law and Disciplinary Power' (2000) 48 *The Sociological Review* 283, 284.

14 Gary Wickham, 'Foucault and Law', in *An Introduction to Law and Social Theory*, ed. Reza Banakar and Max Travers (Oxford: Hart, 2002), pp. 249–65 (p. 249).

15 See Michel Foucault (ed.), *I, Pierre Rivière, having slaughtered my mother, my sister, and my brother … : A Case of Parricide in the 19th Century*, trans. Frank Jelinek (New York: Pantheon, 1975); Michel Foucault, *Abnormal: Lectures at the Collège de France 1974–1975*, trans. Graham Burchell (London: Verso, 2003), especially the first six lectures of the collection.

16 As our later discussion of Foucault will demonstrate, such a neat distinction between exegesis and application cannot actually be sustained either conceptually or in practice. However, the distinction serves a useful heuristic function at this stage in our argument, as indeed it has for others. See Jonathon Simon, '"In Another Kind of Wood": Michel Foucault and Sociolegal Studies' (1992) 17 *Law and Social Inquiry* 49, 49–50; Baxter, 'Bringing Foucault into Law and Law into Foucault', pp. 450–51.

17 For example, see Mark Barenberg, 'Democracy and Domination in the Law of Workplace Cooperation: From Bureaucratic to Flexible Production' (1994) 94 *Columbia Law Review* 753.

18 For example, see Christine Bateup, 'Power v the State: Some Cultural Foucauldian Reflections on Administrative Law, Corporatisation and Privatisation' (1999) 3 *Southern Cross University Law Review* 85.

19 For example, see Kendall Thomas, 'Beyond the Privacy Principle' (1992) 92 *Columbia Law Review* 1431.

20 For example, see Tony Evans, 'International Human Rights Law as Power/Knowledge' (2005) 27 *Human Rights Quarterly* 1046.

21 For example, see Nickolas James, 'Power-Knowledge in Australian Legal Education: Corporatism's Reign' (2004) 26 *Sydney Law Review* 587.

22 Michel Foucault, 'Powers and Strategies', in *Power/Knowledge*, pp. 134–45 (p. 145).

23 For some well argued and well founded reservations on this score, see Baxter, 'Bringing Foucault into Law and Law into Foucault', pp. 473–79.

24 For the most important example, see Jacques Derrida, 'Force of Law: The "Mystical Foundation of Authority"', trans. Mary Quaintance, in *Acts of Religion*, ed. Gil Anidjar (New York: Routledge, 2002), pp. 228–98.

25 For example, see Margrit Shildrick, 'Transgressing the Law with Foucault and Derrida: Some Reflections on Anomalous Embodiment' (2005) 47 *Critical Quarterly* 30; Friedrich Balke, 'Derrida and Foucault on Sovereignty' (2005) 6 *German Law Journal* 71; Mariana Valverde, 'Derrida's Justice and Foucault's Freedom: Ethics, History, and Social Movements' (1999) 24 *Law and Social Inquiry* 655; Daniel Williams, 'Law, Deconstruction and Resistance: The Critical Stances of Derrida and Foucault' (1988) 6 *Cardozo Arts and Entertainment Law Journal* 359. Although for a contrary view, see Richard Warfield, 'Considering an Exercise of Self and Justice in the Later Foucault' (1999) 18 *Carleton University Student Journal of Philosophy* (accessed online at: http://www.carleton.ca./philosophy/cusjp/v18/n1/warfield. html).

26 Cf. specifically the disagreement between Foucault and Derrida, surrounding the latter's reading of Foucault's *Histoire de la folie* – see Roy Boyne, *Foucault and Derrida: The Other Side of Reason* (London: Routledge, 1990). Foucault's text was originally published in 1961 as *Folie et Déraison*. *Histoire de la folie à l'âge classique*. *Folie et Déraison* was then re-released in abridged paperback form in France in 1964. The initial English translation by Richard Howard was of this much-shortened text, with some material from the longer French original which Foucault had restored. See Michel Foucault, *Madness and Civilization: A History of Insanity in the Age of Reason*, trans. Richard Howard (London: Routledge, 1967). In 1972, Foucault published a second edition of the entire book (with some appendices) as *Histoire de la folie à l'âge classique*. A new English translation has recently been issued of this full edition: Michel Foucault, *History of Madness*, trans. Jonathan Murphy and Jean Khalfa (Abingdon: Routledge, 2006). Derrida's initial critique of *Histoire de la folie* was given in the form of a lecture on 4 March 1963 which was subsequently published as 'Cogito and the History of Madness', trans. Alan Bass, in *Writing and Difference* (London: Routledge, 2001), pp. 36–76. For Foucault's straitened reply, see 'My Body, This Paper, This Fire', in *Essential Works of Foucault 1954–1984, Vol. 2: Aesthetics, Method, and Epistemology*, trans. Robert Hurley et al., ed. James Faubion (Harmondsworth: Penguin, 2000), pp. 393–417. Foucault also published a separate text in February 1972 entitled 'Reply to Derrida', which is reproduced as an appendix to the recently translated *History of Madness* (at pp. 575–90).

Chapter 1

Orientations: Foucault and law

> One's first book is read, because one isn't known, because people don't know who one is, and it is read in disorder and confusion, which suits me fine. There is no reason why one should write not only the book, but also lay down the law as to how it should be read. The only such law is that of all possible readings.[1]

As we intimated in our Introduction, and as Foucault's generous law of readership would itself imply, our exercise in re-reading Foucault is not intended as a rejection of what has come before us. Accordingly, we are not arguing in this book that all previous readings of Foucault's stance on law are 'wrong' or not textually justified. Rather, we are arguing that previous interpretations of Foucault do indeed capture something of his stance on law, but fail to account for – and thence to connect – crucial dimensions of his thought. What we argue in this book is that Foucault illustrates two salient dimensions of law which, when brought together, result in a nuanced and radical theory of law. Our re-reading of Foucault's law is thus in large part an exercise in refinement, and extension, of previous interpretations but one which nevertheless results in a reversal of them. In what follows we discuss some of the existing readings of Foucault's treatment of law in order to set the account which we offer in Chapters 2 and 3 of the book. In the first section of the present chapter we address the 'orthodox' interpretation of Foucault's stance on law that we have been discussing up to now. This thesis, most extensively developed by Hunt and Wickham in their book *Foucault and Law*, asserts that Foucault 'expelled' law from his analysis of power relations in modernity by marginalizing it and subordinating it to other modalities of power. In the second section of the chapter, we turn to focus on a number of other rival interpretations which attempt to defend Foucault from the charge that he failed to properly integrate law into his genealogical analyses of the present – these accounts all try, in different ways, to locate Foucault's law within modernity. What we are attempting to do in this chapter is to provide a conspectus of these different readings of Foucault, in order both to draw from them and to depart from them in advancing our own interpretation of Foucault's law.

Alongside our discussion of these varying interpretations of Foucault, we also address a number of well known Foucaultian texts from the mid-1970s which are commonly relied upon by most scholars in formulating their respective positions on Foucault and law: *Discipline and Punish*; the first volume of Foucault's projected six-volume *History of Sexuality*; and the series of interviews, lectures and essays collected in the anthology *Power/Knowledge*. These texts, from the popular 'power analytics', or genealogical, phase of his work, form the basis of most legal interpretations of Foucault and it is thus appropriate that we provide some introduction to them here in order to make sense of these readings of Foucault on law. We should make clear, however, that these texts by no means represent the limits of our own reading of Foucault in this book. In formulating our interpretation of Foucault's law we draw upon a range of other materials, such as: first, some of Foucault's earlier work of the 1960s wherein he engages with several of his literary-philosophical contemporaries (notably, Maurice Blanchot and Georges Bataille); second, some of Foucault's recently published and translated lecture courses at the Collège de France from the 1970s (such as *Abnormal*, *'Society Must Be Defended'* and *Security, Territory, Population*); and, finally, his work of the late 1970s and early 1980s on forms of modern political rationality in the West, on 'governmentality', and on ancient Greek and imperial Roman ethics.[2] The purpose of our discussion in this chapter is thus twofold: first, to sketch in broad outline the divergent readings that his work has provoked (as a preliminary step to advancing our own reading of Foucault in the remainder of this book); and, second, to introduce the reader to some key Foucaultian concepts and important texts from the mid- to late 1970s.

THE 'EXPULSION THESIS'

Arguably the most enduring, though by no means uncontested, reading of Foucault on law is the thesis that he failed to appreciate the importance of law in modernity and indeed expelled it from his analyses of contemporary power relations. As our discussion of the various proponents of this view (and they are many) will show, this interpretation of Foucault is in most instances a *critical* reading of his stance on law. The argument that Foucault failed to take proper account of law's constitutive role in society, or that he offers a straitened portrait of law as a mere instrument of repression which is superseded by more productive and expansive modern modalities of power, has been rehearsed by a number of theorists from a range of different critical positions from the late 1970s until the present day: Nicos Poulantzas, Bob Fine, Paul Hirst, Carol Smart, Duncan Kennedy, Boaventura de Sousa Santos, and several others, have all critiqued Foucault's understanding of law along these, and similar, lines.[3] Whilst we do engage with the views of these theorists in the course of our discussion, the contention that Foucault misconceived, marginalized and expelled law from his critical accounts of modernity finds its most recent and sustained expression in both the sole- and joint-authored work of Alan Hunt and Gary Wickham.[4] Accordingly, we focus our attention upon their work but as our discussion progresses we shall also make reference to the other theorists discussed here.

As we mentioned above, the aim of our discussion in this section is not simply to summarize the argument that Foucault expelled or marginalized law, but also to read some of Foucault's key texts in the process. By thus reading Foucault with (and sometimes against) his critics we hope not only to illustrate the 'expulsion thesis' but also to give a brief introduction to some important Foucaultian concepts central to an understanding of his thought and to our interpretation of him. Accordingly, alongside our discussion of the 'expulsion thesis' we include direct references to Foucault's texts themselves (in part to illustrate and animate this reading of him, in part to offer some general introductory material). We shall now begin to address the 'expulsion thesis' in more detail.

At its core, the argument that Foucault expelled law can be reduced to the thesis that in a series of texts from the mid- to late 1970s in which he outlines his radical conception of power relations Foucault identifies law and sovereignty with a pre-modern form of negative, repressive power which is progressively overtaken by a new mode of operation, or technology, of power, namely disciplinary power. According to this reading of Foucault, the emergence of the new disciplinary power marks the historical transition to a modernity wherein the old forms of law and sovereignty become decreasingly important as a site, and mode of operation, of power. Even with the publication of the first volume of *The History of Sexuality* in 1976, so goes the argument, in which Foucault adds to his concept of an individualizing disciplinary power over bodies the concept of a bio-power over populations, the law and forms of sovereign power are very much attenuated in their effectiveness and application. Enter power (in various guises); exit law.[5] Foucault, on this reading of him, renders law as an instrument of repression, control and social ordering which is overtaken by more expansive modes of power. Law remains only to perform a residual role of instrument or accessory to such now predominant powers of modernity.

On this reading of Foucault, importantly, the nature and form of the new disciplinary and bio-political modes of power are largely incompatible with the old forms of law and sovereignty. While the former, in Foucault's by-now-famous formulation, are variously positive, productive, continuous and dispersed throughout the social body,[6] the latter are repressive, deductive, violent and occasional in their operation, tied to the sclerotic form of the centralized state apparatus and thoroughly inefficient as a means of surveilling and correcting individual bodies or managing populations.[7] The transition to modernity, in this quite standard reading of Foucault, thus effects both a qualitative and a quantitative break in terms of the operation of power in society. Power is now exercised not through the ponderous forms of law or juridical mechanisms with their pre-modern ties to monarchical sovereignty, but rather via the new institutional forms of power he calls the disciplines, or through the assertion of power over whole populations he comes to identify as bio-power (of which disciplinary power forms one axis). Furthermore, whilst Foucault does not assert that the law and its associated juridical forms simply wither away entirely in modernity, nevertheless they do cease to perform any meaningful role. In an early statement of this reading, Nicos Poulantzas observed that:

> Foucault is led to underestimate at the very least the role of law in the exercise of power within modern societies; but he also under-estimates the role of the State itself, and fails to understand the function of the repressive apparatuses (army, police, judicial system, etc.) as means of exercising physical violence that are located at the heart of the modern State. They are treated instead as mere parts of the disciplinary machine which patterns the internalization of repression by means of normalization.[8]

Bob Fine and Paul Hirst decry Foucault's alleged subsuming of law within an ever-expanding disciplinary network in similar terms (which are quite representative of the 'expulsion thesis'). For example, Fine contends that Foucault sees law as entirely subordinated to disciplinary power, with discipline 'reign[ing] supreme'[9] over an ineffective law; whilst Hirst reads Foucault as saying that law is 'no more than a rubber stamp that sanctions the functioning of [the] disciplinary system'.[10] In such terms is Foucault alleged to have downgraded the law's central importance in modernity, instrumentally subordinating it to the insinuative demands of an ineluctably expanding disciplinary/bio-political matrix which maps the social body in its entirety. As we shall see, this reading of Foucault maintains that he saw law as being: essentially negative (and violent) in its mode of operation; historically tied to monarchical sovereignty; and, finally, with the transition to modernity, overtaken by more productive and effective technologies of power which invest it and instrumentally subordinate it to their operations. We discuss each of these aspects in turn as we seek to build up a picture of the 'expulsion thesis'.

There is certainly much textual warrant within Foucault's works from the mid- to late 1970s for the 'expulsion thesis' we have just outlined. An apt place in which to commence this engagement is in Foucault's critique of what he calls the 'juridico-discursive' conception of power, as this is the context in which a great deal of Foucault's comments on law are made. As Foucault puts it in the first volume of *The History of Sexuality*, describing the purported operation of a juridico-discursive operation of power as it relates to sexuality:

> [P]ower acts by laying down the rule: power's hold on sex is maintained through language, or rather through the act of discourse that creates, from the very fact that it is articulated, a rule of law. It speaks, and that is the rule. The pure form of power resides in the function of the legislator; and its mode of action with regard to sex is of a juridico-discursive character.[11]

According to this common understanding of power, power is exercised in a fundamentally negative fashion. Power lays down a rule which demarcates the licit from the illicit, seeking to repress and negate that which it prohibits. In Foucault's view, such a juridico-discursive conception of power elides the crucial point that power is in fact not negative and repressive but rather productive, or formative. Power does not operate on a pre-given object but in fact functions to produce that very object. As Foucault argues, famously, in *Discipline and Punish*:

> We must cease once and for all to describe the effects of power in negative terms: it 'excludes', it 'represses', it 'censors', it 'abstracts', it 'masks', it 'conceals'. In fact, power produces; it produces reality; it produces domains of objects and rituals of truth.[12]

We shall take up in a moment an example of what Foucault intends when he argues that power is productive when we look at the question of disciplinary power and the formation of the subject. However, if we focus for the meantime on law and its claimed relation to the juridico-discursive conception of power, we can see that in places Foucault does apparently equate law itself with a narrow conception of power – as a limit which simply says 'Thou shalt not'. Discussing law's supposed relation to sexuality, in Volume 1 of *The History of Sexuality*, Foucault remarks in characteristic terms:

> [T]hou shalt not go near, thou shalt not touch, thou shalt not consume, thou shalt not experience pleasure, thou shalt not speak, thou shalt not show thyself; ultimately thou shalt not exist, except in darkness and secrecy. To deal with sex, power employs nothing more than a law of prohibition. Its objective: that sex renounce itself. Its instrument: the threat of a punishment that is nothing other than the suppression of sex.[13]

As the book's argument makes abundantly clear, this is not Foucault's understanding of the complicated relationship between *power* and sexuality. That understanding is figured, rather, as a positive and productive relationship. Nevertheless, the point is that here (and elsewhere) Foucault does seem to want to circumscribe the role of *law* (a particular form of power) as being pre-eminently negative and as functioning within a very restricted juridico-discursive economy. Law is conceived of as 'a law which says no'[14] and as 'the law of prohibition'.[15] It is 'essentially',[16] indeed 'excessively',[17] repressive in its mode of operation. Moreover, and importantly for Foucault, this 'somber law that always says no'[18] is not just a negative power but ultimately an abidingly limited one as well (which helps explain, on this reading, its historical eclipse in modernity by more insidious, efficient and expansive forms of power). Thus, we see Foucault describe the juridical apparatus as limited to 'simple and endlessly reproduced mechanisms'.[19] Such is the 'poverty and monotony of interdictions'[20] that they are unable to reach down into the fine-grained depths and details of the modern social body. It is worth quoting at greater length from the first volume of *The History of Sexuality* once more to emphasize Foucault's argument that law as negative sanction is inherently limited in its scope and application:

> Underlying both the general theme that power represses sex and the idea that the law constitutes desire, one encounters the same putative mechanics of power. It is defined in a strangely restrictive way, in that, to begin with, this power is poor in resources, sparing of its methods, monotonous in the tactics it utilizes, incapable of invention, and seemingly doomed always to repeat itself. Further, it is a power that only has the force of the negative on its side, a power to say no; in no condition to produce, capable only of posting limits, it

is basically anti-energy. ... And finally, it is a power *whose model is essentially juridical, centred on nothing more than the statement of the law* and the operation of taboos.[21]

Again, while in the quotation above Foucault may well be attacking a certain juridico-discursive conception of *power*, the important point to note for our purposes is that he does talk of such an understanding of power in terms of its being *legal*, as if law actually functioned in this manner, as if law were, as he says above, 'capable only of posting limits'. For Foucault, it appears from these texts, law does simply represent an 'instance of negation',[22] and it is no doubt statements such as these which have prompted theorists such as Duncan Kennedy to label Foucault a 'criminalist' in his imperative understanding of law,[23] and Hunt and Wickham, for example, to argue that Foucault's 'inadequate conception of law' excludes a richer consideration of law's constitutive capacities.[24] Hirst also interprets Foucault as arguing that law is nothing but 'limit or prohibition, whereas disciplinary power transforms and magnifies the capacities of the subjects on which it works'.[25]

If law is a purely negative, and it seems inherently limited, mechanism, it is also fading in importance as a historical means of exercising power – for this reading of Foucault on law maintains not simply that he characterizes law as a negative force of repression but that he sees it as entering into an almost terminal decline with the advent of modernity. Writing of the way in which the monarchical states of the Middle Ages had historically established control over local, warring factions through the use of law, Foucault observed:

> Doubtless there was more to this development of great monarchic institutions than a pure and simple juridical edifice. But such was the language of power, the representation it gave of itself, and the entire theory of public law that was constructed in the Middle Ages, or reconstructed from Roman law, bears witness to the fact. Law was not simply a weapon skillfully wielded by monarchs; it was the monarchic system's mode of manifestation and the form of its acceptability. In Western societies since the Middle Ages, the exercise of power has always been formulated in terms of law.[26]

Hunt and Wickham criticize Foucault here for making the narrow and historically inaccurate claim that law simply represented the sovereign's will, arguing that Foucault fails to account for other, dispersed sources of legality.[27] But this is not all. This law, which we have seen Foucault characterize as negative, repressive and limited, was in the hands of the monarch also an extremely violent power which was exercised only occasionally to cow his subjects into obedience. The opening pages of *Discipline and Punish*, wherein Foucault recounts the public ordeal of Damiens the regicide, or the passage where he quotes at some length from Brantôme's account of the eighteen-day torture of the assassin of William of Orange in 1584,[28] are just two of his more famous (and harrowing) examples of this sovereign violence enacted through law. We might also recall Foucault's evocation of law in the essay 'Nietzsche, Genealogy, History', a piece which manifests the great influence that Nietzsche had upon his historiographical method.[29] There, in terms very much reminiscent of Nietzsche, he describes the law as:

> [T]he calculated pleasure of relentlessness. It is the promised blood, which permits the perpetual instigation of new dominations and the staging of meticulously repeated scenes of violence.[30]

However, this form of sovereign power, in which an enraged king exacted murderous vengeance for offences against the law through the (in)judicious deployment of an occasional violence was – according to Foucault's broad historical claim – superseded in the eighteenth century by another type of power. This type of power was a technology much more finely calibrated than the brute instrument of law as wielded by the monarch transgressed. To the 'majestic rituals of sovereignty' and its law were opposed the 'humble modalities' and 'minor procedures' of this emergent technology.[31] Here we begin to see power's productivity. Foucault again, this time from the lecture course *Abnormal*:

> There was the elaboration of what could be called a new economy of the mechanisms of power: a set of procedures and analyses that enabled the effects of power to be increased, the costs of its exercise reduced and its exercise integrated in mechanisms of production. By increasing the effects of power I mean that there was the discovery in the eighteenth century of a number of means by which, or at least, the principle in accordance with which power could be exercised in a continuous manner, rather than in the ritual, ceremonial, discontinuous way it was exercised under feudalism and continued to be exercised in the absolute monarchies. That is to say, it is no longer exercised through ritual, but through permanent mechanisms of surveillance and control.[32]

The 'economy of power' which Foucault is discussing in the above lecture of 29 January 1975 will be familiar to many readers as his concept of disciplinary power, a concept which he developed most extensively in *Discipline and Punish*. In the prison, the factory workshop, the school, the barracks and the asylum, this new economy of power worked to 'fabricate'[33] subjects in modernity not through the direct imposition of physical violence but rather through the more subtle repetition of forms of graduated exercise and daily routine. It was in these various institutional locations, which in the modern age betrayed a telling isomorphism,[34] that power functioned to discipline individuals according to relevant behavioural norms (the productive worker, the assiduous student, the dutiful child, and so forth) and to insert these individuals into modes of production. Through constant and studied repetition these norms were internalized by the individual and manifested in his or her conduct. The important point to note, for our present purposes, is that it was not by resort to supposedly juridical mechanisms that the resultant compliant subject, the 'docile body' in Foucault's terms,[35] was forged. Rather, the constitution of the modern subject of discipline was achieved through new and different techniques – spatial distributions, hierarchical observations, normalizing judgments, constant surveillance and examinations (with their petty penalties and forced exercises).[36]

Foucault discusses a number of different disciplinary techniques but perhaps the most telling mechanism was Jeremy Bentham's architectural design of the Panopticon.[37] Here is a description of the model from *Discipline and Punish*:

> [A]t the periphery, an annular building; at the centre, a tower; this tower is pierced with wide windows that open onto the inner side of the ring; the peripheric building is divided into cells, each of which extends the whole width of the building; they have two windows, one on the inside, corresponding to the windows of the tower; the other, on the outside, allows the light to cross the cell from one end to the other. All that is needed, then, is to place a supervisor in a central tower and to shut up in each cell a madman, a patient, a condemned man, a worker or a schoolboy. By the effect of backlighting, one can observe from the tower, standing out precisely against the light, the small captive shadows in the cells of the periphery. They are like so many cages, so many small theatres, in which each actor is alone, perfectly individualized and constantly visible. The panoptic mechanism arranges spatial unities that make it possible to see constantly and to recognize immediately. In short, it reverses the principle of the dungeon; or rather of its three functions – to enclose, to deprive of light and to hide – it preserves only the first and eliminates the other two. Full lighting and the eye of a supervisor

capture better than darkness, which ultimately protected. Visibility is a trap.[38]

'[T]he major effect of the Panopticon,' argues Foucault, is 'to induce in the inmate a state of conscious and permanent visibility that assures the automatic functioning of power.'[39] In the panoptic disciplinary regime, power functions all the more effectively through its not actually needing to be enforced – it is automatic in that the individual to be disciplined automatically assumes that the guard in the tower is watching, and modifies his or her behaviour accordingly. In the above long quotation from *Discipline and Punish*, Foucault also argues that the Panopticon 'reverses the principle of the dungeon'. More importantly, the Panopticon actually produces a more fundamental reversal. This is the reversal of what Foucault calls 'the political axis of individualization'. Foucault explains elsewhere in *Discipline and Punish* that:

> The disciplines mark the moment when the reversal of the political axis of individualization – as one might call it – takes place. In certain societies, of which the feudal régime is only one example, it may be said that individualization is greatest where sovereignty is exercised and in the higher echelons of power. The more one possesses power and privilege, the more one is marked as an individual, by rituals, written accounts or visual reproductions. ... In a disciplinary régime, on the other hand, individualization is 'descending': as power becomes more anonymous and more functional, those on whom it is exercised tend to be more strongly individualized; it is exercised by surveillance rather than ceremonies, by observation rather than commemorative accounts, by comparative measures that have the 'norm' as reference rather than genealogies giving ancestors as points of reference.[40]

Whilst under disciplinary conditions the schoolboy, the patient, the soldier or the prisoner is enjoined to perform an homogenizing norm, the specification of the disciplinary gaze actually practises a greater individualization of the subject of discipline. Individuals are turned into 'cases' and their relative distance from the norm is ranked hierarchically in the disciplinary regime.

This quintessentially modern form of power, which aimed to punish subjects not so much for transgressions of a pre-given law, but rather for failure to attain an evolving and immanent normality, functioned in a positive and productive manner. In this way, individuals are seen by Foucault as a product of disciplinary power: 'The individual is no doubt the fictitious atom of an "ideological" representation of society; but he is also a reality fabricated by this specific technology of power that I have called "discipline".'[41] And again, Foucault writes that: 'it is not that the beautiful totality of the individual is amputated, repressed, altered by our social order, it is rather that the individual is carefully fabricated in it, according to a whole technique of forces and bodies'.[42]

In formulating his concept of a disciplinary power which produced the subject upon which it acted through the articulation of a norm,[43] Foucault was attempting to isolate a modality of power which exceeded the logic of the state and which transcended the usual theatres of state power.[44] He was searching for the exercise of power in places where political theorists of the state had not been wont to look – in the interstices of the disciplinary regime; in the workplace, the asylum, and so forth. In Foucault's words, he was searching for power's effects 'at its extremities, at its outer limits at the point where it becomes capillary'.[45] In Foucault's formulation, then, discipline was a diffuse power which through its mundane attention to the minutiae of the quotidian could infinitely 'extend beyond the limits of the State' and its law.[46]

Foucault would later supplement this formulation of a disciplinary power of normalization with an account of a different technology of power, in the first volume of *The History of Sexuality* – a technology of power he was to label 'bio-power'. Whereas disciplinary power focused upon the individual body in need of correction, bio-power was focused not at the level of the individual but rather at the level of the population or the species as a whole.[47] And whereas the old sovereign power of the monarch, exercised through a vengeful and violent law, represented a power of 'deduction *(prélèvement)*, a subtraction mechanism, a right to appropriate a portion of the wealth, a tax of products, goods and services, labor and blood, levied on the subjects',[48] bio-power, like disciplinary power, was an innately productive mechanism. It fostered and managed life. Indeed, for Foucault, bio-power constituted nothing less than the entry of life into the order of politics – the emergence of a 'society in which political power had assigned itself the task of administering life'.[49] In the age of bio-power, according to Foucault, the well-being of the population became an explicit object of political attention such that elements like 'propagation, births and mortality, the level of health, life expectancy and longevity, with all the conditions that can cause these to vary' became subject to governmental intervention, management and regulatory control.[50] With Foucault's elaboration of bio-power,[51] we see – at 'micro' and 'macro' levels, so to speak – the joint articulation of the two technologies of power. As Foucault puts it, an '*anatamo-politics of the human body*' (disciplinary power) becomes linked to a '*bio-politics of the population*' (bio-power) and their combined aim is to endow and utilize life.[52]

To return our discussion more closely, though, to the place of law – and more accurately, to the (receding) place of law in the 'expulsion thesis' – we can see once again that Foucault does intimate in places that the role of law in the new disciplinary and bio-political configuration of modernity is somewhat attenuated, to say the least. In the first volume of *The History of Sexuality*, for example, he observes that:

> We have been engaged for centuries in a type of society in which the juridical is increasingly incapable of coding power, of serving as its system of representation. Our historical gradient carries us further and further away from a reign of law that had already begun to recede into the past at a time when the French Revolution and the accompanying age of constitutions and codes seemed to destine it for a future that was at hand.[53]

Indeed, in the same work, he talks in terms of our entering a 'phase of juridical regression' characterized by 'the growing importance assumed by the action of the norm, at the expense of the juridical system of the law'.[54] If Foucault is insistent that the law and juridical institutions still remain in place ('I do not mean to say that the law fades into the background or that the institutions of justice tend to disappear'),[55] then what, exactly, is the fate of law in modernity? It is here that Foucault is most (interestingly) conflicted. As we shall see, many advocates of the 'expulsion thesis' do acknowledge the several different formulations of law's relationship to discipline or bio-power offered by Foucault, and in this regard they are attentive to the nuance of his thought. Nevertheless, what unites these readers is their contention that, for Foucault, regardless of the precise relationship between law and the new forms of modern power, law is marginalized and rendered increasingly irrelevant in modernity where what is needed is a more expansive and pervasive form of power. In making this contention they would ultimately assimilate Foucault's equivocations to a univocal narrative of law's demise.

Turning now to this question of the relationship between law and disciplinary power, we see that in places Foucault articulates what Duncan Kennedy calls the 'radical discontinuity' between,[56] and Boaventura de Sousa Santos terms the 'mutual incompatibility' of,[57] legal-juridical power and disciplinary power. In 'The Eye of Power', for example, Foucault describes the new panoptic disciplinary surveillance as 'exactly the opposite of [a] monarchical power'[58] which operates through law; and in *Discipline and Punish* he describes the disciplines as actually constituting a 'counter-law'.[59] In *Security, Territory, Population* Foucault explains that, 'the problem that [he is] trying to mark out is how techniques of normalization develop from and below a system of law, in its margins and maybe even against it'.[60] He renders the opposition between disciplinary normalization and legality in even stronger terms in *'Society Must Be Defended'*, contending that 'this type of power [disciplinary power] is the exact, point-for-point opposite of the mechanics of power that the theory of sovereignty described'[61] – a theory of sovereignty which represented, for Foucault, a 'system of Law-and-Sovereign'.[62] In functional terms, Foucault stresses in *'Society Must Be Defended'*, such a disciplinary power was 'absolutely incompatible with relations of sovereignty' mediated through law.[63] Foucault continues in this way:

> The discourse of discipline is alien to that of the law; it is alien to the discourse that makes rules a product of the will of the sovereign. The discourse of disciplines is about a rule: not a juridical rule derived from sovereignty, but a discourse about a natural rule, or in other words a norm. Disciplines will define not a code of law, but a code of normalization, and they will necessarily refer to a theoretical horizon that is not the edifice of law, but the field of the human sciences. And the jurisprudence of these disciplines will be that of a clinical knowledge.[64]

If in the above instances Foucault is concerned to maintain a conceptual and practical distinction between disciplinary power and sovereign-legal power, if not in fact to establish the absolute irreducibility of the two economies of power, nevertheless in other places he stresses their symbiosis and mutual interaction, and the necessary relations between the law and the modalities of power outside it. For example, in the same piece just quoted, Foucault remarks that, '[s]overeignty and discipline, legislation, the right of sovereignty and disciplinary mechanics are in fact the two things that constitute – in an absolute sense – the general mechanisms of power in our society',[65] and he writes elsewhere of the 'communication between the power of discipline and the power of the law'.[66] There is thus something of an irresolution on Foucault's part here with respect to his placing of law within the new disciplinary or bio-political configuration of modernity. On the one hand he would seem to counterpose the old forms of sovereignty and law to the new modalities of power (indicating that the latter are outstripping the former); on the other, he would seemingly gesture towards their interaction or mutual articulation. We want to return to this irresolution in later chapters, in which we will argue that Foucault's seeming uncertainty (and this uncertainty is identified by some of his readers but its theoretical implications are left unexamined and undeveloped) is in fact revealing of a much more radical and indeed coherent theorization of law.

While some readings of Foucault which argue that he marginalized the role of law simply interpret him as having completely subjugated law to discipline or bio-power (such as those of Bob Fine and Paul Hirst),[67] others do draw attention to this irresolution on Foucault's part. Hunt and Wickham rightly observe that Foucault's treatment of law is conflicted, representing a 'determined separation of law and disciplines followed by partial retreats',[68] and de Sousa Santos acknowledges that Foucault's position on the relation of law to the new technologies of power is, if not nuanced or interestingly fraught, at any rate 'confusing'![69] Nevertheless, what unites the readings of Foucault which we have been discussing here is their assertion that, on the whole, Foucault 'refuses to accord any major role to legal regulation in creating the distinctive features of modernity'.[70] These readings of Foucault point to passages where, regardless of the opposition or interaction of law and discipline, the law is either rendered as an institutional support for the disciplinary network or its very being is challenged, indeed invaded, by the new powers. For example, Foucault writes in Volume 1 of *The History of Sexuality* that 'the law operates more and more as a norm, and that the judicial institution is increasingly incorporated into a continuum of apparatuses (medical, administrative, and so on) whose functions are for the most part regulatory'.[71] In *Discipline and Punish* we see a similar formulation, where he argues that the disciplines 'gradually ... invade the major [legal] forms, altering their mechanisms and imposing their procedures',[72] whilst, finally, in *'Society Must Be Defended'*, Foucault continues the invasion/colonization metaphor by suggesting that 'the techniques of discipline and discourses born of discipline are invading right, and that normalizing procedures are increasingly colonizing the procedures of the law'.[73] Where the law retains some separate form of existence in these passages, it is relegated very much to a supporting role, either masking or legitimating the material, corporeal work of the disciplines. Ironically, given Foucault's often gymnastic attempts to circumvent the Marxian problematic of ideology and (false) consciousness,[74] such descriptions look suspiciously like an epiphenomenal or superstructural law mystifying a 'real' disciplinary enslavement.[75] As he puts it in *Discipline and Punish*:

> Historically, the process by which the bourgeoisie became in the course of the eighteenth century the politically dominant class was masked by the establishment of an explicit, coded and formally egalitarian juridical framework, made possible by the organization

of a parliamentary, representative régime. But the development and generalization of disciplinary mechanisms constituted the other, dark side of these processes. The general juridical form that guaranteed a system of rights that were egalitarian in principle was supported by these tiny, everyday, physical mechanisms, by all those systems of micro-power that are essentially non-egalitarian and asymmetrical that we call the disciplines ... [and which] provide, at the base, a guarantee of the submission of forces and bodies. The real, corporal disciplines constituted the foundation of the formal, juridical liberties.[76]

In summarizing this particular reading of Foucault, then, we can see that despite in places acknowledging the complexities in his work and the contradictory formulations of law, discipline, and bio-power contained therein, the general trend and impetus of the interpretations we have discussed in this section are to read Foucault as having downgraded, marginalized or expelled the law. Foucault's law, according to the 'expulsion thesis', is both limiting and (historically) limited; a form of negative power which he assimilates to monarchical sovereignty and then summarily deposes with the coming of modernity, relegating it to a subordinate and thoroughly contained position. If law 'lingers on'[77] in the present it is as an anachronism of an age gone by, or in the guise of instrument, accessory or support for more insidious and pervasive forms of disciplinary or bio-political power. As we have seen, there is no shortage of textual support for this reading in Foucault's work, particularly in several works from the mid- to late 1970s. It would indeed seem difficult, in the face of bare pronouncements like 'law recedes'[78] in modernity and statements that we have entered into a period of 'juridical regression',[79] to find a generative place for law within Foucault's thought. And yet, as the readings we discuss in the remainder of this chapter (and our own, developed at greater length in Chapters 2 and 3) demonstrate, there is ample scope for a very different view of Foucault's position on law.

RETRIEVING/RE-READING FOUCAULT

As we intimated at the beginning of the previous section, the 'expulsion thesis' reading of Foucault, whilst perhaps being the most common understanding of how he figured law, is by no means the only way in which he has been interpreted. Indeed, the thesis that Foucault left law out of account has been contested in a number of different ways by a number of different theorists: some hinting at a more nuanced interrelation of law and discipline, or law and bio-power, running throughout his thought; some attempting to recuperate Foucault's treatment of law by reading later works *against* the works of his middle period to thereby supplement a supposed lack in his engagement with law; and others making an argument about Foucault's use of the word 'juridical' (and its nonequivalence with the terms 'law' and 'legal'). These interpretive strategies all share a concern to foreground the law in Foucault's work, and to argue that he did not omit it from his reflections on modernity. Many of the writers whose work we discuss below articulate these three different lines of argument together or in combination, and they are certainly interrelated in several important respects, but our aim being as it was in the above section (namely, to survey the respective ways of interpreting Foucault's conflicted stance on law and to provide some reference to his texts in so doing), we discuss the arguments sequentially for the sake of clarity. We have endeavoured to extract representative passages of the general arguments rather than discuss every proponent of each argument. As will become evident in succeeding chapters, we draw from components of these readings in constructing our own reading of Foucault on law. In doing so we take most from the first reading we discuss here, and as our discussion in Chapter 2 will make clear, we believe there is much room to develop the insights of this particular strand of interpretation. The final two interpretations we discuss, in attempting to read law back into Foucault, actually rehearse some of the same critical gestures of the 'expulsion thesis' and end by confining Foucault's law and assimilating it to the emergent forms of rule in modernity rather than recuperating it. Let us now examine these three related interpretations in turn.

Discipline and law

Against the reading of Hunt and Wickham, and many others, discussed in the previous section, several commentators have raised the objection that Foucault does not in fact place disciplinary power in opposition to the law (and subordinate the latter to the former in so doing). Rather, Foucault actually describes how law and discipline are interrelated and are deployed jointly in modernity. Anthony Beck, in a critical engagement with the central thesis of Hunt and Wickham's *Foucault and Law*, points out that '[d]iscipline in contrast to law is [their] principal theme'.[80] According to Beck, it is this (false) antinomy that permits the authors to attribute an expulsion of law to Foucault, when in fact '[l]aw is not excluded by the disciplines, the two are interdependent'.[81] Beck continues in this vein:

Foucault's argument is first, that modern order and power is [*sic*] comprised of the two systems of state-law on the one hand and the disciplines on the other. Secondly, the ubiquitous democratic characterisation of law, and the rule of law, has masked the real importance of control of the populace through the disciplines. It is not the case that he argues that law is simply a mask; it is both a mask and a real source of power, at least of equal importance to the disciplines.[82]

Thus, discipline *and* law, and not discipline *in contrast to* law, is Beck's way of reading Foucault – and it is one which is shared by several other critics.[83] For example, Nikolas Rose and Mariana Valverde identify a 'co-existence, hybridization and mutual inter-dependence of law and norm' in Foucault's thought,[84] and Duncan Ivison is in agreement with them, urging the kind of Foucaultian legal interpretation and scholarship that would 'separate, without collapsing, "techniques of juridical rule" from "techniques of the norm" as a way of analysing the role of law in modern societies'.[85] Beck proposes one possible example of the interaction between law and discipline when he argues that, 'the constitution of an effective disciplinary space as such rests upon law, upon property and contract, whether it is in the prison, the school, hospital or work-place, as does the relationship of the parties involved in that space'.[86] So, on this view, law, which is anterior to disciplinary power, facilitates the operation of the latter by constituting spaces which are then traversed and invested by the disciplines.

Turning to Foucault's lecture course *Abnormal*, we find a neat illustration of this kind of enabling relay between law and disciplinary power (in this particular case, psychiatric power). In his lecture of 12 February 1975, Foucault discusses the effects of an 1838 law regulating the making of hospitalization orders (the confinement of the insane in psychiatric hospitals). According to Foucault, by defining in law the 'specialized medical character' of the confinement, '[t]he 1838 law consecrated psychiatry as a medical discipline, but also as a specialized discipline within the field of medical practice'.[87] Moreover, in reorienting the line of psychiatric enquiry from a concern with the subject's mental capacity to a concern with the subject's potential to cause public disturbance and disrupt social order, the 1838 law also 'sanction[ed] the role of psychiatry as a particular scientific and specialized technique of public hygiene'.[88] Thus, we can see how law in this instance both enabled the operation of psychiatric power by establishing it as a medical discipline and also impacted upon the functioning of psychiatric power by posing new questions (which allowed both the domain and the influence of psychiatric power to widen and grow). Far from receding in importance, then, the law in modernity comes to be ever more constantly involved in deploying and harnessing the disciplines – a kind of constitutive compatibility of law and discipline. That is, as one of Foucault's collaborators puts it in a joint interview from 1978, 'it is quite possible to believe that traditional repressive laws will function side-by-side with much more subtle forms of control'.[89]

Another possible way to read the relation between law and discipline in Foucault's work is that the former acts to constrain the depredations of the latter – an *agonistic* relation as opposed to one of *compatibility*, yet one still characterized by the persistence of law in some form. Typically, commentators on Foucault, critical both of his seeming lack of faith in the emancipatory potential of legal discourse[90] and of his belief that law becomes increasingly incapable (whatever its emancipatory pretensions) of restraining an expansive disciplinary power,[91] point to his advice at the end of the second lecture of *'Society Must Be Defended'* that, 'if we are to struggle against disciplines, or rather against disciplinary power, in our search for a nondisciplinary power, we should not be turning to the old right of sovereignty'.[92] For example, both Hunt and Wickham and Kirstie McClure argue that Foucault tends (in this passage and elsewhere in his work) to elide the political potential of rights claims.[93] Interestingly, however, Jan Goldstein argues that there *is* room in Foucault for a reading of law as providing some kind of restraint upon disciplinary power, however attenuated.[94] Relying upon passages in Foucault's 1977 piece, 'About the Concept of the "Dangerous Individual" in Nineteenth-Century Legal Psychiatry',[95] Goldstein argues that Foucault's position on the 'merits of law in relation to discipline was ... more ambiguous, iridescent, and ... intellectually interesting' than such commentators would allow,[96] and that at least in this piece we can see Foucault acknowledging (and applauding) the law's refusal to accept, from the late nineteenth century to the 1970s, the disciplinary discourses of criminal anthropology and forensic psychiatry which sought to institute a kind of 'social defence' against the 'dangerous individual'. We might perhaps read in a similar light some of Foucault's later journalistic texts, such as 'Useless to Revolt?', 'The Moral and Social Experience of the Poles Can No Longer be Obliterated' and 'Confronting Governments: Human Rights',[97] in which there is a redeployment of rights discourse in the form of a *right of the governed*, which right can act as a restraint upon governmental power.[98]

We engage with the question of rights in Chapter 3. However, in concluding our brief sketch of this line of argument, we can see that one possible way to defend Foucault from the charge that he has omitted law from his investigation of modernity is to argue that far from erroneously counterposing law and discipline, and relegating the former to the role of institutional support or mere accessory of the latter, he in fact in some places envisioned their interaction, overlapping and mutual articulation, and, in others, described their tension and ongoing confrontation. This relation between law and discipline, between law and the power that in a way lies outside it, is something which is central to our own re-reading of Foucault's law. Such a line of argument is, for us, a most illuminating way to start re-reading Foucault and we seek to build upon and refine its insights in the chapters that follow.

The governmentality of law

Thus far, we have mainly been focusing on Foucault's work of the mid-1970s on disciplinary formations. The second possible counter-reading of Foucault on law (and again, we should stress that these avenues of reading are by no means mutually exclusive) is one which focuses upon the work presented or published after the first volume of *The History of Sexuality*. This work comprises, most notably, Foucault's examination of governmentality and his discussion of modalities of liberal rule and political rationality (often, along with the second and third volumes of *The History of Sexuality* and his work on ancient Greek ethics, compendiously referred to as 'the late Foucault').[99] To be fair to the main proponents of the 'expulsion thesis', Hunt and Wickham, this is a body of published work which they themselves identify as a potential means to make good the omissions of Foucault's earlier work on 'power analytics' of the mid-1970s, thus constituting something of a self-correction on Foucault's part (although, as we shall see, this revelation does not betoken a simple reintroduction of law). Nevertheless it is in this work, contend Hunt and Wickham, that 'the earlier expulsion of law from modernity is significantly modified'. In that work, Foucault properly begins to address 'the purposive rationality of the legislative output of representative legislatures' and at last recognizes the 'increasing particularism of regulatory instruments'.[100] A supposed (re)turn to law, then.

The best-known piece of this period is Foucault's lecture entitled 'Governmentality'. Given that it has inspired a wide range of related research projects and is the piece most engaged with in terms of the material we are about to discuss,[101] the lecture probably merits a short summary at this point. This will also help us better identify the (shifting) place of law within Foucault's governmental horizon of the late 1970s and early 1980s.[102] It is first necessary, however, to place 'Governmentality' within the wider context of Foucault's work at the time (including the series of lectures of which it was originally a part) and to situate it within his important shift from an emphasis upon discipline and the subjection of individuals to a concern with the problematics of government and the way in which subjects in modernity are increasingly led to govern themselves outside of institutions. The lecture was delivered in February 1978 as part of Foucault's course at the Collège de France for the academic year 1977–78: *Security, Territory, Population*.[103] In the lecture course as a whole, Foucault traces the rise of a form of power he labels pastoral power, the origins of which lie in the Hebraic and Eastern Christian religions (as opposed to the political culture of classical Greece in which the trope of the leader as pastor or shepherd was much less noticeable or important, according to Foucault).[104] This modality of pastoral power is appropriated, intensified and massively elaborated by the Western Church in the form of the Christian pastorate from the third century onwards, but, importantly, after the Reformation, elements of pastoral power become gradually taken up and assimilated by putatively 'secular' state modalities of rule (such as the doctrine of *raison d'État* or the German science of *Polizeiwissenschaft*, or, simply, *police*).[105] Foucault's lecture course is hence the narrative of the progressive 'secularization' of the Christian pastorate and the adoption of many aspects of pastoral power by the institutions of the modern European nation-state.[106]

Foucault characterizes the political technology of pastoral power in the following way: first, it was exercised over a flock of people on the move rather than over a static territory; second, it was a fundamentally beneficent power according to which the duty of the pastor (to the point of self-sacrifice) was the salvation of the flock; and finally, it was an individualizing power, in that the pastor must care for each and every member of the flock singly.[107] As Foucault observes, '[t]he pastor must really take charge of and observe daily life in order to form a never-ending knowledge of the behaviour and conduct of the members of the flock he supervises'.[108] Crucially, the pastor's concern with the everyday behaviour of his charges must also extend to the 'spiritual direction' (*direction de conscience*) of the thoughts of his flock – a procedure which involves the production and extraction of 'a truth which binds one to the person who directs one's conscience'.[109] Foucault illustrates a model of power, then, in which there is a complex (and thoroughly affective) tie between the pastor who exercises a minute and careful jurisdiction over the bodily actions and the souls of his flock in order to assure their salvation, and each member of the flock who must owe him 'a kind of exhaustive, total, and permanent relationship of individual obedience'.[110] As Foucault's historical narrative unfolds in *Security, Territory, Population*, we can trace a shift from the pastoral care of a flock in early Christian models of the pastorate to the governmental management of a population in modern state formations, or from the pastoral promise of spiritual salvation to the pastoral promise of material salvation within the frame of the modern administered state. 'In a way,' Foucault argues elsewhere, 'we can see the state as a modern matrix of individualization, or a new form of pastoral power.'[111]

Foucault's concept of governmentality has both a general and a specific meaning. At its most general, governmentality simply refers to any manner in which people think about, and put into practice, calculated plans for governing themselves and others. In this respect, the early form of the pastorate discussed in lectures five, six and seven of *Security, Territory, Population* is an example of governmentality in that the pastor practises a form of government (linked to a precise and meticulous knowledge) of his flock, whilst members of the flock practise a certain government of themselves through their examination of themselves and their consciences.[112] However, the more specific meaning of the term governmentality, and the one which has influenced most scholars, is the particular form of governmentality that Foucault discusses in the fourth lecture of the course and which, as we have noted above, was published separately as 'Governmentality'.

This more specific understanding of governmentality refers to a particular mode of deploying and reflecting upon power (like Foucault's earlier identification of disciplinary power and bio-power as modalities of power) developed by certain political theorists from the middle of the sixteenth to the end of the eighteenth century. These political theorists were attempting to distance themselves from a Machiavellian conception of power, understood as a sovereign's retaining control over his or her territory. In developing a counter-Machiavellian 'art of government', these writers expounded a non-sovereign 'kind of rationality which was intrinsic to the art of government, without subordinating it to the problematic of the prince and of his relationship to the principality of which he is lord and master'.[113] What was important for these theorists was not the maintenance of a transcendent and singular sovereign power over a principality but rather the care and maximization of the potential of the *population* itself (and in this can be discerned the pastoral roots of this manner of thinking about and exercising power). Population becomes the political object of governmentality, with a specific density of its own, and it is towards the population that the techniques of the art of government must adapt themselves and upon which they must bring themselves to bear: 'It [the population] is a set of elements in which we can note constants and regularities even in accidents ... and with regard to which we can identify a number of modifiable variables on which it depends.'[114] In the words of the sixteenth-century author

Guillaume de La Perrière, the 'art of government' concerned 'the right disposition of things arranged so as to lead to a suitable end',[115] and this end was the constant improvement of the population, the maximization of its health, well-being, material prosperity, and so forth, through tactical regulatory interventions:

> The things government must be concerned about, La Perrière says, are men in their relationships, bonds, and complex involvements with things like wealth, resources, means of subsistence, and, of course, the territory with its borders, qualities, climate, dryness, fertility, and so on. 'Things' are men in their relationships with things like customs, habits, ways of acting and thinking. Finally, they are men in their relationships with things like accidents, misfortunes, famine, epidemics, and death.[116]

Now, this concept of governmentality bears marked similarities to the notion of bio-power introduced by Foucault in the final chapter and final lecture, respectively, of the first volume of *The History of Sexuality* and *'Society Must Be Defended'*.[117] Both refer to a manner of exercising power over a population that is directed towards maximizing its potential and optimizing its capacities, yet Foucault never to our knowledge explicitly discusses the relationship between the two concepts. We read the difference as being largely one of emphasis and of detail: first, governmentality, and the shift that the concept introduces into Foucault's thinking with the idea of a government of oneself, imports a greater emphasis upon those governmental strategies that function by inciting subjects to govern themselves (the use of technologies of the self);[118] then, second, the concept of governmentality provides a more precise historical example (through the writings of political theorists and the concrete practices of political rule) of the rather broad (and relatively underdeveloped) notion of a bio-political management of life.[119]

Importantly, as Foucault remarks, the modern state still functions according to this dispositional and technocratic logic of governmentality: '[w]e live in the era of a governmentality' characterized by a '"governmentalization" of the state'.[120] In Foucault's account, what is of central importance is not the state *per se* but rather the fact that the modern state has come to function according to this new modality of power called governmentality:[121]

> By this word 'governmentality' I mean three things. First, by 'governmentality' I understand the ensemble formed by institutions, procedures, analyses and reflections, calculations, and tactics that allow the

exercise of this very specific, albeit very complex, power that has the population as its target, political economy as its major form of knowledge, and apparatuses of security as its essential technical instrument. Second, by 'governmentality' I understand the tendency, the line of force, that for a long time, and throughout the West, has constantly led towards the pre-eminence over all other types of power – sovereignty, discipline, and so on – of the type of power that we can call 'government' and which has led to the development of a series of specific governmental apparatuses (*appareils*) on the one hand, [and, on the other] to the development of a series of knowledges (*savoirs*). Finally, by 'governmentality' I think we should understand the process, or rather, the result of the process by which the state of justice of the Middle Ages became the administrative state in the fifteenth and sixteenth centuries and was gradually 'governmentalized'.[122]

Whilst the above formulation of the different modalities of power gives the impression that sovereignty is replaced by discipline which is in turn replaced by a technocratic governmentality with its statistical modulation and management of the population, Foucault makes clear elsewhere in the lecture that governmentality as a form of power operates alongside the disciplines:

> So we should not see things as the replacement of a society of sovereignty by a society of discipline, and then of a society of discipline by a society, say, of government. In fact we have a triangle: sovereignty, discipline, and governmental management, which has population as its main target and apparatuses of security as its essential mechanism.[123]

It is this impulse in Foucault's work on governmentality, this triangulation of the different modalities of power, which has convinced scholars such as Nikolas Rose and Mariana Valverde, for example, that at least in this period of his work Foucault meant to imply the interrelation and co-implication of legal, disciplinary and governmental strategies. On this reading the 'legal complex', far from receding in importance, is in fact integrated into governmental strategies and forms a central part of the isolation and management of social problems by the government.[124] Law becomes a part of the wider dispersal of governmental sites and functions throughout the social body. Similarly, Marianne Constable, in her analysis of the interrelation of the modalities of sovereign power and governmentality in the context of modern American immigration law, shows (following Foucault) how the laws generated by modern states are in the nature of '"policies" – regulations concerned with order at the level of populations and their individual components and informed by the regularities and interests depicted by human sciences'.[125] We might think not only of immigration laws but also of laws regulating the provision of health, welfare and housing benefits, of laws governing health and safety requirements and (rather obvious candidates for inclusion) laws relating to in vitro fertilization, human embryo usage, and so forth. So law here, in these readings of Foucault, forms a central part of the governmental armoury, along with the disciplinary matrix and the requisite 'knowledges of man' generated by the emergent human sciences.

This does on one view, however, entail a subtle change in the nature of law, as Foucault explains in the fourth lecture of *Security, Territory, Population*:

> Here, on the contrary, it is not a matter of imposing a law on men, but of the disposition of things, that is to say, of employing tactics rather than laws, or, of as far as possible *employing laws as tactics*; arranging things so that this or that end may be achieved through a certain number of means.[126]

We can discern in this quotation the contours of precisely the kind of law which Hunt and Wickham (and others) have criticized as being instrumentally subordinated to the imperatives of modern power. Law in the horizon of governmentality appears to retain some effectivity but is arguably refigured as a tactical component of an overriding governmental-administrative apparatus. It is possible to read this deployment of law not (as per Rose and Valverde, and Constable, above) as a reintegration of law in modernity but rather as an assimilation of law to governmental or administrative imperatives, which is broadly analogous to Foucault's earlier alleged subsuming of law to disciplinary power or bio-power. Indeed, despite the indications that law has a constitutive role to play in modernity, Foucault's work on governmentality and political rationality characteristically eludes a straightforward reading as the narrative of law's belated return. Rather, we might trace in this work a narrative of law's abject doubling – as either the blunt, vicious and antiquated tool of sovereignty (against which the model of *law as governmentality* is set), or the pliant instrument of a tactical administration to which we are consigned in the present.

The work on governmentality and law which we have addressed in this section has the merit of demonstrating how law remains a part of Foucault's critical account of modernity. However, what it fails to address is precisely the tension and ambivalence between modes of legality and modes of administration and governmentality, and in so doing it fails to grasp something of the 'specificity'[127] of law's relationship with these new modes of power – law simply becomes one of the many different aspects of our late modern administered world and is thus in a way subsumed by the techniques of governmentality.[128] We hope in the ensuing chapter to demonstrate something of the complex relation between law and the forms of power which lie outside or beyond it.

The 'juridical' and the 'legal'

Finally, the last attempt to (re)locate the legal within Foucault's thought that we consider in this chapter is the argument that, simplifying somewhat, the terms 'juridical' (or juridico-discursive) and 'legal' are not synonymous in Foucault's usage. As we shall see, this line of critique has a semantic point of departure yet aims, ultimately, to advance a broader conceptual thesis about the nature of modern law and its relation to normalizing practices. We find the argument first propounded by Foucault's former colleague and assistant at the Collège de France, François Ewald. The latter begins his article 'Norms, Discipline, and the Law' by returning to the scene of one of Foucault's more memorable rhetorical denunciations of law and sovereignty – the final chapter (entitled 'Right of Death and Power over Life') of the first volume of *The History of Sexuality*. In this final chapter, Foucault, it would seem, commits the law to an early grave on the brink of modernity. We have already seen how Foucault links the rise of bio-power to a correlative process of 'juridical regression'.[129] In Foucault's reckoning, the historical expanse of a power over life is set inversely to the decline of a right of death,[130] that is, bio-power increasingly inhabits the space vacated by the juridical. And it is precisely this figure of 'the juridical' to which Ewald has recourse in exhuming a hastily interred law from Foucault's account. 'Foucault does not mean to suggest here that the development of bio-power is accompanied by a decline of law,' Ewald observes.[131] In marked contrast to many of the theorists we have been discussing throughout this chapter, Ewald argues that:

> [Foucault's] further commentary makes it clear that the formation of a normalizing society in no way diminished the power of law or caused judicial institutions to disappear. In fact, normalization tends to be accompanied by an astonishing proliferation of legislation. ... The norm, then, is opposed not to law itself but to what Foucault would call 'the juridical': the institution of law as the expression of

a sovereign's power. If, as Foucault puts it, 'the law cannot help but be armed,' and if its weapon *par excellence* is death, this equation of law and death does not derive from the essential character of the law. Law can also function by formulating norms, thus becoming part of a different sort of power that 'has to qualify, measure, appraise, and hierarchize rather than display itself in its murderous splendor.' In the age of bio-power, the *juridical*, which character-ized monarchical law, can readily be opposed to the *normative*, which comes to the fore most typically in constitutions, legal codes, and 'the constant and clamorous activity of the legislature'.[132]

So, in detaching the juridical from the legal, Ewald makes the argument that Foucault's real target was never the latter *per se* but rather the former, conceived here by Ewald as 'the institution of law as the expression of a sovereign's power'.[133] On Ewald's view, once we recognize the distinc-tion between the juridical and the legal, we are able to perceive that for Foucault the more important distinction is in fact the divide between two ways of representing or understanding the operation of law: the juridical and the normative. These are, Ewald contends, implacably opposed in Foucault's thought. Furthermore, we are told, the law can (and increasingly does) operate according to the logic of the norm and not pursuant to an antediluvian juridical logic of desire, command and threatened sanction. Far from narrating the demise of 'law and legality in modern society',[134] Ewald's Foucault gestures towards an incipient *normative law* in modernity. Indeed, as Foucault himself writes in Volume 1 of *The History of Sexuality*, in the age of bio-power 'the law operates more and more as a norm'.[135] The object of Foucault's critique thus becomes those who would maintain that law still operates according to a juridical formula (in Foucault's terms, 'the juridical is increasingly incapable of coding power, of serving as its system of representation').[136] What Foucault is saying, according to Ewald, is that in modernity the juridical is an inappropriate means of representing and understanding law, and that in fact law exceeds the juridical economy to which it is wrongly assigned: the law becomes disciplinary and bio-political.[137]

Ewald's reading of Foucault has proved quite influential with Fou-caultian legal scholars. Victor Tadros, for example, has built upon Ewald's distinction between the juridical and the legal and argued for its importance in grasping Foucault's conception of modern power relations. Tadros extends Ewald's formulation by arguing that the juridical was not simply a code or way of representing power but rather a 'particular network of power; a real set of power relations which are connected together in a particular form'.[138] On this reading, then, we must distinguish between the law, the network of power relations, and, lastly, the code or the means by which power (re)presents itself.[139] The warning against eliding the legal with the juridical in Foucault's thought has also found some purchase in feminist-oriented critiques (which engage with Carol Smart's reading of Foucault on law in her *Feminism and the Power of Law*)[140] and also, finally, in some of the critiques inspired by Foucault's work on governmentality to which we have previously adverted.[141] These readings all share a concern to reinstate the law in Foucault's work and, in emphasizing that according to Foucault the juridical mode of power is on the decline, to show how the law functions in a bio-political manner through the norm – a slide from the law of the rule to the law of the norm.

And yet, for all the neatness of these readings, and granted their apt intent to resituate the law in interpretations of Foucault, they do lose something of the specificity of the law in Foucault's account (admittedly such specificity is not often perceived, but this perception is in part what we are setting out to achieve in this book). Rather like the readings discussed above which take their point of departure from Foucault's work on governmentality, these interpretations actually end in occluding that which they seek to highlight and retrieve. Putting aside for the moment those places in Foucault's texts where a distinction between the legal and the juridical (upon which, it will be remembered, this reading rests) would seem to be foreclosed,[142] we want to finish this section by showing how a reading of law *as* norm, in Foucault's sense, fails to capture law's dimensions adequately.

In 'Norms, Discipline, and the Law', Ewald makes an interpretive argument about Foucault's understanding of law. In a related body of work, Ewald builds upon his interpretation of Foucault in order to construct a concept of 'social law'. We address these writings on 'social law' in Chapter 3 in much more depth and from a different perspective, but here we are primarily interested in how Ewald's formulation of 'social law' reveals how his interpretation of Foucault results in a subsumption of the law by the norm and a failure to articulate the complex interrelation between the two which, as we have seen, Foucault wanted to maintain. Let us now look at this notion of 'social law' which Ewald articulates in a number of different texts.[143]

Social law, Ewald argues, is 'the term for the legal practices that typify the Welfare State'.[144] The emergence and development of principles of social law are not, he tells us, confined to labour and social security law. Rather, revealing a penchant for macro-historical categorization somewhat reminiscent of his former mentor, Ewald's social law constitutes nothing other than 'a new legal system'.[145] The advent of the welfare state ushers in a new type of legal system and a new way of conceiving of legality which is not based upon the imposition of abstract universal principles but rather upon the use of the law 'as an [sic] political instrument, as an instrument of government'[146] in the temporary resolution of social conflicts over, for example, resource allocation and access to political processes. Social law is not concerned with defining universal principles of right but rather with balancing the partial and contesting rights claims of members of a political community, and in doing so it has resort, perforce, to the norm:

> One term sums up the whole set of characteristics of this logic of legal judgment: the term *norm*. A judgment of balance, in the social law sense, is a *normative* judgment. Judging in terms of balance means judging the value of an action or a practice in its relationship to social normality, in terms of the customs and habits which at a certain moment are those of a given group.[147]

In the concluding analysis, indeed on the final page of his article 'A Concept of Social Law', Ewald justifies his notion of social law by recourse to Foucault. Quoting a phrase from the first volume of *The History of Sexuality*, Ewald writes: 'The passage from classical law to social law should, then, be analysed as the passage "from the Law to the norm".'[148] Ultimately, despite Ewald's efforts to articulate the norm with legal concepts of judging, balancing and justice, we read the attempt to construct a new principle of social law as simply replicating the gesture – for which, as we have seen, Foucault has himself been criticized – of subordinating law to the norm, disciplinary power, and the human sciences (see for example Foucault's comment, discussed above, that 'normalizing procedures are increasingly colonizing the procedures of the law').[149] By trying to forge a Foucaultian jurisprudence based around the norm and by arguing that the law functions according to the norm, Ewald ultimately ends by assimilating the law to the norm. In so doing he does not, as Ivison enjoins us to do, 'separate' but in fact 'collaps[es], "techniques of juridical rule" ... [and] "techniques of the norm"'.[150] The overall trend of Foucault's work is, as we have seen, to establish a difference between these different techniques. Most commentators, following Hunt and Wickham, argue that Foucault has not simply separated the two forms of rule but has in fact prioritized the one over the other, but in attempting to argue that some form of Foucaultian legality persists, Ewald has eviscerated the distinction. In our reading of Foucault's law we argue for a more nuanced understanding of law that does not equate law and norm and that acknowledges their constitutive differences. What we are interested in capturing, and what we base our discussion of Foucault's law upon in Chapter 2, is the articulation of law with the modalities of disciplinary power and bio-power that lie both within and outside it.

CONCLUSION

Our aim in this chapter has been to introduce the reader to a number of the different ways of interpreting Foucault's position on law (and to provide some, albeit brief, exposition of a number of key Foucaultian concepts in the process, such as disciplinary power, bio-power and governmentality). Of course, to talk in determinate terms of Foucault's 'position' implies some kind of conceptual stasis or fixity, when in fact Foucault's attitude to law as it emerges from the accounts of the various interlocutors we have been discussing here seems to vacillate between, on the one hand, subordinating and confining the law, and, on the other, reframing it and hinting at its continuing relevance to modernity in some form. What distinguishes our account of Foucault's law from the ones we have been discussing throughout this chapter – both the 'expulsion thesis' and those readings which, in various ways, seek to renovate a seemingly threadbare Foucaultian law – is that we locate Foucault's law in a way that incorporates this irresolution. We locate Foucault's law between a subordinated law and a surpassing law, between a law which is confined by the emerging modalities of disciplinary power and bio-power and one which is illimitable and always going beyond itself and those who would seek to instrumentalize it. It is in the seeming inconsistency between these two different facets of law that Foucault is in fact saying something entirely consistent – and very apposite – about law. Far from trying to tame Foucault's apparently unruly thought, which shifts from position to position, we aim to derive a theory of Foucault's law from this very shifting of positions. The result is a law which, if it is to 'be', must incipiently be ever beyond itself. Our first task, however, is to illustrate in some of Foucault's texts the dimension of law we have only been hinting at so far in this chapter – the idea of law as being illimitable and responsive. This is what we now focus upon in Chapter 2.

Notes

1 Michel Foucault, 'An Aesthetics of Existence', in *Politics, Philosophy, Culture: Interviews and Other Writings, 1977–1984*, trans. Alan Sheridan *et al.*, ed. Lawrence D. Kritzman (London: Routledge, 1988), pp. 47–53 (p. 52).

2 We reference these texts in full later in the chapter when we consider them in greater depth.

3 These authors will all be discussed when we engage with them specifically, below.

4 For the fullest expression of the argument, see Alan Hunt and Gary Wickham, *Foucault and Law: Towards a Sociology of Law as Governance* (London: Pluto Press, 1994). See also Alan Hunt, 'Foucault's Expulsion of Law: Toward a Retrieval' (1992) 17 *Law & Social Inquiry* 1, which is reproduced under the same title as Chapter 12 in his *Explorations in Law and Society: Toward a Constitutive Theory of Law* (London and New York: Routledge, 1993), pp. 267–302; Alan Hunt, 'Law and the Condensation of Power' (1992) 17 *Law & Social Inquiry* 57; Alan Hunt, 'Getting Marx and Foucault into Bed Together!' (2004) 31 *Journal of Law and Society* 592; Gary Wickham, 'Foucault, Law, and Power: A Reassessment' (2006) 33 *Journal of Law and Society* 596; Gary Wickham, 'Foucault and Law', in *An Introduction to Law and Social Theory*, ed. Reza Banakar and Max Travers (Oxford: Hart, 2002), pp. 249–65.

5 It is notable that most readings of Foucault along the lines we have indicated above rely on a relatively limited *corpus* of Foucaultian texts (one which we try to expand in this book) ending with the first volume of *The History of Sexuality* and some of his work on 'governmentality'. There is not a great engagement in the legal literature with the second and third volumes of the *History of Sexuality* project and Foucault's conceptualization of ethics, for example. So, when Gerald Turkel argues that '*The History of Sexuality* is Foucault's last major work', the context of his discussion makes it abundantly clear that he is referring to the first volume only. This is fairly representative of legal engagements with Foucault's work, which confine themselves to his mid-1970s work. See Gerald Turkel, 'Michel Foucault: Law, Power, and Knowledge' (1990) 17 *Journal of Law and Society* 170, 187. In the present setting, given that we are engaging with critical interpretations of Foucault's work which focus on these texts, we shall largely confine ourselves to discussing his mid-1970s work. However, towards the end of this chapter we do engage with Foucault's work on governmentality and political reason, and in our final chapter we seek to demonstrate that Foucault's late work on ethics actually provides a model of law's sociality. For the late work on ethics, see Michel Foucault, *The Use of Pleasure: The History of Sexuality, Vol. 2*, trans. Robert Hurley (Harmondsworth: Penguin, 1992) First published in French by Editions Gallimard, 1984; Michel Foucault, *The Care of the Self: The History of Sexuality, Vol. 3*, trans. Robert Hurley (Harmondsworth: Penguin Books, 1990) First published in French by Editions Gallimard, 1984.

6 For example, see Michel Foucault, *Discipline and Punish: The Birth of the Prison*, trans. Alan Sheridan (Harmondsworth: Penguin, 1991), pp. 194, 297.

7 For example, see Michel Foucault, *The Will to Knowledge: The History of Sexuality, Vol. 1*, trans. Robert Hurley (Harmondsworth: Penguin, 1979), pp. 135–40. For further discussion, see note 52, below.

8 Nicos Poulantzas, *State, Power, Socialism*, trans. Patrick Camiller (London: Verso, 2000), p. 77.

9 Bob Fine, *Democracy and the Rule of Law: Liberal Ideals and Marxist Critiques* (London and Sydney: Pluto Press, 1984), p. 200.

10 Paul Q. Hirst, *Law, Socialism and Democracy* (London: Allen & Unwin, 1986), p. 49.

11 Foucault, *The History of Sexuality, Vol. 1*, p. 83.

12 Foucault, *Discipline and Punish*, p. 194.

13 Foucault, *The History of Sexuality, Vol. 1*, p. 84.

14 Michel Foucault, 'Truth and Power', in *Power/Knowledge: Selected Interviews and Other Writings 1972–1977*, trans. Colin Gordon *et al.*, ed. Colin Gordon (Brighton: Harvester Press, 1980), pp. 109–33 (p. 119).

15 Michel Foucault, 'Powers and Strategies', in *Power/Knowledge*, pp. 134–45 (p. 139).

16 Foucault, 'Truth and Power', p. 122.

17 Foucault, *The History of Sexuality, Vol. 1*, p. 48.

18 *Ibid.*, p. 72.

19 *Ibid.*, p. 84.

20 Foucault, *The History of Sexuality, Vol. 2*, p. 250.

21 Foucault, *The History of Sexuality, Vol. 1*, p. 85 (our emphasis).

22 Foucault, 'Powers and Strategies', p. 140.

23 Duncan Kennedy, 'The Stakes of Law, or Hale and Foucault!', in his *Sexy Dressing Etc.* (Cambridge, MA: Harvard University Press, 1993), pp. 83–125 (p. 119). Although note that Foucault also repeatedly refers to contract and contractualist understandings of law in his writings. For example, see Foucault, *Discipline and Punish*, pp. 169, 222; Michel Foucault, 'About the Concept of the "Dangerous Individual" in Nineteenth-Century Legal Psychiatry', in *Essential Works of Foucault 1954–1984, Vol. 3: Power*, trans. Robert Hurley *et al.*, ed. James D. Faubion (New York: New Press, 2000), pp. 176–200 (pp. 196–200) (on the effect of civil law upon penal law).

24 Hunt and Wickham, *Foucault and Law*, p. 60.

25 Paul Hirst, 'Law, Socialism and Rights', in *Radical Issues in Criminology*, ed. Pat Carlen and Mike Collison (Oxford: Martin Robertson, 1980), pp. 58–105 (p. 92).

26 Foucault, *The History of Sexuality, Vol. 1*, p. 87.

27 Hunt and Wickham claim that Foucault's linking of law to sovereignty is historically unwarranted and that such a move elides the diverse sources and uses of law as 'emanating from dispersed sites of royal power, popular self-regulation, customary rights, competing specialised jurisdictions (ecclesiastical, guild, commercial, etc.), local and regional autonomies, and other forms of law' (*Foucault and Law*, p. 60). Although see Foucault, *Discipline and Punish*, pp. 78–79, where he does acknowledge the many 'discontinuities, overlappings and conflicts between the different legal systems [of the King, the nobility, those administered by governmental or police authorities, and so forth]' which '[b]y their very plethora ... were incapable of covering the social body in its entirety'. For an analogous comparative historical criticism of Foucault's position on law as it pertains to the example of Imperial and Soviet Russia, see Laura Engelstein, 'Combined Underdevelopment: Discipline and the Law in Imperial and Soviet Russia' (1993) 98 *American Historical Review* 338.

28 Foucault, *Discipline and Punish*, pp. 3–6, 54.

29 See also Michel Foucault, 'Prison Talk', in *Power/Knowledge*, pp. 37–54 (pp. 53–54); Michel Foucault, 'Truth and Juridical Forms', in *Essential Works of Foucault, Vol. 3: Power*, pp. 1–89 (pp. 6–15).

30 Michel Foucault, 'Nietzsche, Genealogy, History', in *Essential Works of Foucault 1954–1984, Vol. 2: Aesthetics, Method, and Epistemology*, trans. Robert Hurley *et al.*, ed. James Faubion (Harmondsworth: Penguin, 2000), pp. 369–91 (p. 378).

31 Foucault, *Discipline and Punish*, p. 170.
32 Michel Foucault, *Abnormal: Lectures at the Collège de France 1974–1975*, trans. Graham Burchell (London: Verso, 2003), p. 87.
33 Foucault, *Discipline and Punish*, p. 308.
34 *Ibid.*, pp. 209–16. Foucault maintained that despite their ostensible differences, there was a fundamental correspondence between the ways in which these various institutions subjected the individuals in their 'care'/charge such that 'prisons resemble factories, schools, barracks, hospitals, which all resemble prisons' (*ibid.*, p. 228). Here, as elsewhere, we encounter Foucault's tendency to maintain, on the one hand, the dispersed and autonomous nature of the disciplines, and, on the other, to insist upon their almost totalizing aggregation in something like a 'disciplinary society'. On this, see his Solzhenitsyn-inspired metaphor of the 'carceral archipelago' (*ibid.*, p. 297).
35 *Ibid.*, pp. 135–69. The language used above (of 'forging' or 'fabricating' subjects) may give the impression that for Foucault the subject was a complete effect of power, something totally constituted and determined by discursive or power relations external to the self. Certainly, Foucault was throughout his work concerned to disrupt Enlightenment notions of coherent and autonomous subjectivity, and there are moments, especially in *Discipline and Punish*, when he does seem to reduce subjectivity to an effect of power relations. For example, he writes on p. 305 of that text that, '[k]nowable man (soul, individuality, consciousness, conduct, whatever it is called) is the object-effect of this analytical investment, of this domination-observation' (see also p. 194 of the same text for a similar formulation). However, it is important to note that Foucault's notion of subjectivity was always somewhat more nuanced than such a view would allow. In his later works, such as the second and third volumes of the unfinished *History of Sexuality* project, we see what many commentators term a 'turn to the subject', wherein he is more concerned with how individuals actively create, or constitute, themselves as subjects (Barry Smart, 'On the Subjects of Sexuality, Ethics, and Politics in the Work of Foucault' (1991) 18 *boundary 2* 201). However, even in the middle, or 'power analytics', phase of his work, most conspicuously in *Discipline and Punish* and the first volume of *The History of Sexuality*, it would not be accurate to say that the subject was always acted upon and never acting. Indeed, it is central to Foucault's concept of 'subjection' that the subject 'becomes the principle of his own subjection': 'He who is subjected to a field of visibility, and who knows it, assumes responsibility for the constraints of power; he makes them play spontaneously upon himself; he inscribes in himself the power relation in which he simultaneously plays both roles; he becomes the principle of his own subjection' (*ibid.*, pp. 202–03). Thus, although at this point of his work Foucault underplays this aspect of subjection, there must necessarily be some part of the subject able to stand apart, as it were, and to integrate and bring to bear upon itself in some way the diverse demands of disciplinary power. As Foucault says in a late work: 'It [the subject] is a form, and this form is not primarily or always identical to itself. You do not have the same type of relationship to yourself when you constitute yourself as a political subject who goes to vote or speaks at a meeting and when you are seeking to fulfill your desires in a sexual relationship. ... In each case, one plays, one establishes a different type of relationship to oneself' (see Michel Foucault, 'The

Ethics of the Concern of the Self as a Practice of Freedom', in *Essential Works of Foucault 1954–1984, Vol. 1: Ethics, Subjectivity and Truth*, trans. Robert Hurley *et al.*, ed. Paul Rabinow (Harmondsworth: Allen Lane/Penguin, 1997), pp. 281–301 (p. 290)). Now, the diverse types of disciplinary power which go to constitute us as voting subjects, as subjects of bureaucracy, as desiring sexual subjects, and the like, can obviously in their utter dispersion and irreducibility provide no coherent and unified subjectivity by their own unconcerted motion. Without something more, without the subject's ability to orient and respond to the demands of disciplinary power, the result would be an irredeemably fractured modern subject not fit for disciplinary purpose. Foucault later foregrounds this integrative capacity of the subject in his writings on ethics. We discuss this question again in Chapter 2 in regard to the inability of power to fully comprise the subject. See the text accompanying notes 64–72 in Chapter 2.

36 Part 3 of *Discipline and Punish* provides a fuller explication of the various methods of training, surveillance, and so forth comprised in Foucault's use of the term 'discipline'. See Foucault, *Discipline and Punish*, pp. 135–228.

37 For Foucault, the Panopticon was emblematic of the functioning of the disciplinary regime. Although it was not extensively adopted in practice it served as an ideal model for disciplinary subjection: 'But the Panopticon must not be understood as a dream building: it is the diagram of a mechanism of power reduced to its ideal form; its functioning, abstracted from any obstacle, resistance or friction, must be represented as a pure architectural and optical system: it is in fact a figure of political technology that may and must be detached from any specific use' (*ibid.*, p. 205).

38 *Ibid.*, p. 200.

39 *Ibid.*, p. 201.

40 *Ibid.*, p. 193.

41 *Ibid.*, p. 194.

42 *Ibid.*, p. 217.

43 By 'norm', it should be stressed, Foucault did not mean 'rule' or 'principle'. Indeed, he consistently counterposed his use of the term 'norm' to these legal meanings (for examples, see Foucault, *Abnormal*, p. 50; Michel Foucault, *Security, Territory, Population: Lectures at the Collège de France 1977–78*, trans. Graham Burchell (Basingstoke: Palgrave Macmillan, 2007), p. 56. In the latter example, Foucault discusses, and distinguishes, the positivist jurist Hans Kelsen's use of the term from his own. Besides the fact that norms for Foucault were not explicitly codified, his use of norm differed from what we might call a rule or a principle in several ways: first, a norm is not imposed from outside a social group but is immanent to and arises from their social practices; second, a norm is not concerned with any opposition between legal or illegal, licit or illicit, but rather aims to distribute individuals on a continuum from normal to abnormal (and in this sense we might say that one does not contravene a norm in the way one might contravene a rule – rather, one simply fails to attain a norm); third, there is a sense in which a norm is more formative or constitutive of one's subjectivity than is a rule (that is, one assumes and internalizes a sense of being 'normal' in a way that one does not, supposedly, with legal rules or principles); and, finally, norms are articulated through the human sciences and not through legal institutions.

44 For an interesting comparison of Foucault and Althusser's work on ideolo-gical state apparatuses, see Beatrice Hanssen, *Critique of Violence: Between Poststructuralism and Critical Theory* (London: Routledge, 2000), p. 10.
45 Michel Foucault, *'Society Must Be Defended': Lectures at the Collège de France, 1975–76*, trans. David Macey (London: Allen Lane, 2003), p. 27.
46 Foucault, 'Truth and Power', p. 122.
47 Foucault, *The History of Sexuality, Vol. 1*, p. 137.
48 *Ibid.*, p. 136.
49 *Ibid.*, p. 139.
50 *Ibid.*, p. 139.
51 Given the popularity of recent engagements with the themes of bio-power and bio-politics, it is helpful to distinguish Foucault's usage (as discussed here) from the subsequent deployment of the term by others. The most important recent contribution is that of Giorgio Agamben in his *Homo Sacer* project (most pointedly in his *Homo Sacer: Sovereign Power and Bare Life*, trans. Daniel Heller-Roazen (Stanford, CA: Stanford University Press, 1998)). There, as is becoming increasingly well known, Agamben purports to 'correct' or to 'complete' Foucault's account of modern bio-politics (p. 9). The somewhat indistinct claim to 'correct' or 'complete' Foucault's analysis amounts to two separate yet related assertions: first, that bio-poli-tics is not a modality of power distinct from traditional forms of sover-eignty (as Foucault would have it) but is in fact the 'fundamental activity of sovereign power' (p. 181); and, second, that bio-politics is in fact not a func-tion or effect of modernity but is the 'original political relation' (p. 181) which characterizes Western metaphysics and politics from the time of classical Greece onwards. For a critique of Agamben's reading of Foucault which argues, *inter alia*, that Agamben fails to attend to the nuance of Foucault's position on the relation of sovereign forms of power with bio-power (and replaces this nuanced picture with an impossible sovereignty able to encompass life utterly), see Peter Fitzpatrick, 'Bare Sovereignty: *Homo Sacer* and the Insistence of Law', in *Politics, Metaphysics, and Death: Essays on Giorgio Agamben's* Homo Sacer', ed. Andrew Norris (Durham, NC: Duke University Press, 2005), pp. 49–73 (especially pp. 56–58).
52 Foucault, *The History of Sexuality, Vol. 1*, p. 139 (emphasis in original). However, Foucault does not contend that after the introduction of bio-power the state ceases to kill – rather, the nature of and justifications for this killing are fundamentally altered. Under conditions of bio-power state killing assumes a genocidal or eugenic role such that racialized others are killed for the sake of maintaining the purity of a population. Foucault dis-cusses the centrality, indeed even the indispensability, of racism to state killing under conditions of bio-power in the last lecture of *'Society Must Be Defended'*, pp. 239–63, but then touches on the question only briefly in *The History of Sexuality, Vol. 1*, pp. 137–38, and by the time a similar theme is broached in the lecture course for 1977–78, *Security, Territory, Population*, p. 42, the thematic of race has been dropped entirely. For a discussion of Fou-cault's treatment of racism, see Ann Laura Stoler, *Race and the Education of Desire: Foucault's* History of Sexuality *and the Colonial Order of Things* (Durham, NC: Duke University Press, 1995), pp. 1–94.
53 Foucault, *The History of Sexuality, Vol. 1*, p. 89.
54 *Ibid.*, p. 144.

55 *Ibid.*, p. 144.
56 Kennedy, 'The Stakes of Law, or Hale and Foucault!', p. 117.
57 Boaventura de Sousa Santos, *Toward a New Legal Common Sense: Law, Globalization, and Emancipation*, 2nd edn (London: Butterworths, 2002), p. 5.
58 Michel Foucault, 'The Eye of Power', in *Power/Knowledge*, pp. 146–65 (p. 155).
59 Foucault, *Discipline and Punish*, p. 222.
60 Foucault, *Security, Territory, Population*, p. 56.
61 Foucault, *'Society Must Be Defended'*, p. 36.
62 Foucault, *The History of Sexuality, Vol. 1*, p. 97.
63 Foucault, *'Society Must Be Defended'*, p. 35.
64 *Ibid.*, p. 38.
65 *Ibid.*, p. 39.
66 Foucault, *Discipline and Punish*, p. 303.
67 Fine, *Democracy and the Rule of Law*, p. 200; Hirst, 'Law, Socialism and Rights', p. 91; Hirst, *Law, Socialism and Democracy*, p. 49.
68 Hunt and Wickham, *Foucault and Law*, p. 51.
69 de Sousa Santos, *Toward a New Legal Common Sense*, p. 6. See also Vikki Bell, *Interrogating Incest: Feminism, Foucault and the Law* (London: Routledge, 1993), p. 178: 'Foucault ... seem[s] at times uncertain about whether juridico-discursive power has disappeared, whether it never truly existed (and was just an image projected by those whose power actually operated in different ways) or is still alive and kicking but somewhat subdued by more recent techniques of bio-power.' As George Pavlich astutely observes, writing about the work of Hunt (*Explorations in Law and Society*) and Poulantzas (*State, Power, Socialism*), 'certainly there are passages in Foucault's work that will sustain this ["expulsion thesis"] interpretation. Equally, however, there are moments that indicate a somewhat different reading'. George C. Pavlich, *Justice Fragmented: Mediating Community Disputes under Postmodern Conditions* (London: Routledge, 1996), p. 91.
70 Hunt and Wickham, *Foucault and Law*, p. 48.
71 Foucault, *The History of Sexuality, Vol. 1*, p. 144.
72 Foucault, *Discipline and Punish*, p. 170.
73 Foucault, *'Society Must Be Defended'*, pp. 38–39.
74 For example, see Michel Foucault, 'Body/Power', in *Power/Knowledge*, pp. 55–62 (p. 58); Foucault, 'Truth and Power', p. 118. For a discussion, see David Couzens Hoy, 'Power, Repression, Progress: Foucault, Lukes, and the Frankfurt School', in *Foucault: A Critical Reader*, ed. David Couzens Hoy (Oxford: Blackwell, 1986), pp. 123–47 (pp. 131–34).
75 See Keith Michael Baker, 'A Foucauldian French Revolution?', in *Foucault and the Writing of History*, ed. Jan Goldstein (Oxford: Blackwell, 1994), pp. 187–205 (p. 195). For a more nuanced view of this passage, see Mitchell Dean, 'Normalising Democracy: Foucault and Habermas on Democracy, Liberalism and Law', in *Foucault contra Habermas: Recasting the Dialogue between Genealogy and Critical Theory*, ed. Samantha Ashenden and David Owen (London: Sage, 1999), pp. 166–94 (pp. 170–71).
76 Foucault, *Discipline and Punish*, p. 222. For a similar formulation, see Michel Foucault, 'The History of Sexuality', in *Power/Knowledge*, pp. 183–93 (p. 187).
77 Hunt and Wickham, *Foucault and Law*, p. 56.
78 Foucault, *Security, Territory, Population*, p. 99.
79 Foucault, *The History of Sexuality, Vol. 1*, p. 144.

80 Anthony Beck, 'Foucault and Law: The Collapse of Law's Empire' (1996) 16 *Oxford Journal of Legal Studies* 489, 492.
81 *Ibid.*, p. 493.
82 *Ibid.*, p. 494.
83 There are some accounts of Foucault's work which aim to apply the insight that law and discipline are interrelated categories to a range of different historical and contemporary political configurations. For example, see Margrit Shildrick, 'Transgressing the Law with Foucault and Derrida: Some Reflections on Anomalous Embodiment' (2005) 47 *Critical Quarterly* 30; Miles Ogborn, 'Law and Discipline in Nineteenth Century English State Formation: The Contagious Diseases Acts of 1864, 1866 and 1869' (1993) 6 *Journal of Historical Sociology* 28. These studies argue for a more sophisticated and nuanced understanding of the relationship between law and disciplinary power. However, where these accounts part company from the analyses of scholars such as Rose and Valverde, Ivison and Beck (discussed in the text above) is in their insistence that any complexifying of the relationship between law and disciplinary power is not to be found in Foucault's texts themselves and that Foucault himself failed to develop the relation. For example, see Shildrick, 'Transgressing the Law with Foucault and Derrida', p. 32; Ogborn, 'Law and Discipline in Nineteenth Century English State Formation', p. 32.
84 Nikolas Rose and Mariana Valverde, 'Governed by Law?' (1998) 7 *Social and Legal Studies* 541, 542.
85 Duncan Ivison, 'The Technical and the Political: Discourses of Race, Reasons of State' (1998) 7 *Social and Legal Studies* 561, 562. The internal quotations are taken by the author from *ibid.*, p. 544.
86 Beck, 'Foucault and Law: The Collapse of Law's Empire', p. 498.
87 Foucault, *Abnormal*, p. 140.
88 *Ibid.*, p. 141.
89 Jean Danet, quoted in Michel Foucault, 'Sexual Morality and the Law', in *Politics, Philosophy, Culture*, pp. 271–85 (p. 275).
90 As far as the specific question of whether Foucault's thought can ground a liberatory jurisprudence (and the fairly predictable conclusion that it cannot), see Douglas Litowitz, 'Foucault on Law: Modernity as Negative Utopia' (1995) 21 *Queen's Law Journal* 1.
91 For example, see Carole Smith, 'The Sovereign State v Foucault: Law and Disciplinary Power' (2000) 48 *The Sociological Review* 283, 283–92.
92 Foucault, *'Society Must Be Defended'*, pp. 39–40. Of course, the passage famously continues that ' ... we should be looking for a new right that is both antidisciplinary and emancipated from the principle of sovereignty'. Even sympathetic engagements tend to conclude, as Roger Mourad does, that 'efforts to derive a satisfactory form of individual right from Foucault's critique have not been very successful', largely due no doubt to the fact that 'Foucault himself did not attempt to develop a new form of right' (Roger Mourad, 'After Foucault: A New Form of Right' (2003) 29 *Philosophy & Social Criticism* 451, 456). For an unsympathetic engagement with Foucault's stance on rights, which tries to construct a theory of rights from his call for a new form of right but which ultimately finds Foucault's project (as the author understands it) incoherent, see Brent L. Pickett, 'Foucaultian Rights?' (2000) 37 *The Social Science Journal* 403.

93 For example, Hunt and Wickham argue in *Foucault and Law* that Foucault deploys (in the above passage and elsewhere in his work) a 'slippage from "right" to "rights"' which indissolubly links the latter to the former such that rights cannot function (at least in their 'old' incarnation which Foucault is criticizing in the above quotation) as a principle or mode of political resistance to disciplinary or sovereign power (p. 45, and see also the related discussion on pp. 63–64). Note Hunt and Wickham are here referring to an earlier publication of this passage in Michel Foucault, 'Two Lectures', in *Power/Knowledge*, pp. 78–108 (p. 108). Kirstie McClure makes a related argument that Foucault reads the political potential out of rights discourse. See Kirstie M. McLure, 'Taking Liberties in Foucault's Triangle: Sovereignty, Discipline, Governmentality, and the Subject of Rights', in *Identities, Politics, and Rights*, ed. Austin Sarat and Thomas R. Kearns (Ann Arbor: University of Michigan Press, 1995), pp. 149–92 (p. 171).

94 Jan Goldstein, 'Framing Discipline with Law: Problems and Promises of the Liberal State' (1993) 98 *American Historical Review* 364, 365–70.

95 See note 23 above.

96 Goldstein, 'Framing Discipline with Law', p. 369.

97 These texts are all reproduced in *Essential Works of Foucault, Vol. 3: Power*, at pp. 449–53, 465–73 and 474–75, respectively.

98 There has been some very useful scholarship on the place of human rights in Foucault's philosophy. In addition to the works cited in notes 92 and 93, above, see Tom Keenan, 'The "Paradox" of Knowledge and Power: Reading Foucault on a Bias' (1987) 15 *Political Theory* 5; Duncan Ivison, 'The Disciplinary Moment: Foucault, Law and the Reinscription of Rights', in *The Later Foucault: Politics and Philosophy*, ed. Jeremy Moss (London: Sage, 1998), pp. 129–48.

99 We look in more depth at Foucault's late writings on ancient Greek and imperial Roman ethics in the final section of Chapter 3. What we focus upon in this present section, however, is Foucault's writings on governmentality, forms of political rationality and the political technology of individuals. Along with the key text 'Governmentality' there are a number of important related lectures that Foucault gave in the United States in which he focuses specifically upon the doctrine of *raison d'État* and the science of the *police* (for example, Michel Foucault, 'The Political Technology of Individuals', in *Essential Works of Foucault, Vol. 3: Power*, pp. 403–17; Michel Foucault, '"Omnes et Singulatim": Toward a Critique of Political Reason', in *Essential Works of Foucault, Vol. 3: Power*, pp. 298–325). On the convoluted publication history of these lectures, and for a summary of their contents, see Nancy J. Holland, '"Truth as Force": Michel Foucault on Religion, State Power, and the Law' (2002) 18 *Journal of Law and Religion* 79. See also Michel Foucault, 'The Subject and Power', in *Essential Works of Foucault, Vol. 3: Power*, pp. 326–48, which discusses themes similar to those contained in the American lectures.

100 Hunt and Wickham, *Foucault and Law*, p. 55. While the authors maintain that during this period Foucault's 'account of the place of law is ... more developed' (p. 54), they argue that Foucault did not *fully* develop this line of thought (p. 55). The second part of their book is an attempt to do so. See also Wickham, 'Foucault and Law', pp. 261–65.

101 In particular, see some of the work of Nikolas Rose and Peter Miller, which develops the insights of Foucault's work on governmentality, especially Nikolas Rose, 'The Death of the Social? Re-figuring the Territory of Government'

(1996) 25 *Economy and Society* 327; Peter Miller and Nikolas Rose, 'Governing Economic Life' (1990) 19 *Economy and Society* 1; Nikolas Rose and Peter Miller, 'Political Power Beyond the State: Problematics of Government' (1992) 43 *British Journal of Sociology* 172. These writers focus upon the dispersal of governmental sites and functions in late modern Western capitalist societies (as the title of the last-mentioned article implies, 'beyond the state') after the retreat of Keynesian welfarism and the decentralization of the welfare state in the latter part of the twentieth century. They hence extend Foucault's analysis of liberalism as a political technology, or mode of governmentality, into the domain of contemporary neo-liberalism. This has become a productive strain of Foucault-inspired enquiry. For an informative and representative collection of essays, see *Foucault and Political Reason: Liberalism, Neo-liberalism and Rationalities of Government*, ed. Andrew Barry, Thomas Osborne and Nikolas Rose (London: Routledge, 1996). For a collection featuring similar work which concerns law, see *Rethinking Law, Society and Governance: Foucault's Bequest*, ed. Gary Wickham and George Pavlich (Oxford: Hart, 2001). In this collection, see especially Jo Goodie, 'The Invention of the Environment as a Subject of Legal Governance', pp. 79–91; Kevin Stenson, 'Reconstructing the Government of Crime', pp. 93–108; David Brown, 'Governmentality and Law and Order', pp. 109–21.

102 For a fuller treatment of the theme of governmentality in Foucault's work and its subsequent development by other scholars, see Mitchell Dean, *Governmentality* (London: Sage, 1999).

103 Foucault, *Security, Territory, Population*, pp. 87–114. The lecture was first published in English in the journal *Ideology & Consciousness* in 1979 but was reprinted and revised as Michel Foucault, 'Governmentality', trans. Colin Gordon, in *The Foucault Effect: Studies in Governmentality*, ed. Graham Burchell, Colin Gordon and Peter Miller (Chicago: University of Chicago Press, 1991), pp. 87–104.

104 Foucault, *Security, Territory, Population*, pp. 135–47.

105 By 'police', Foucault does not simply mean a police force entrusted with prosecuting breaches of the criminal law. In his own words: 'The meaning of these German and French words [*police* and *Polizei*] is puzzling since they have been used at least from the nineteenth century until now to designate something else, a very specific institution that, at least in France and Germany – I don't know about the United States – didn't always have a very good reputation. But, from the end of the sixteenth century to the end of the eighteenth century, the words *police* and *Polizei* had a very broad and, at the same time, also a very precise meaning. When people spoke about police at this moment, they spoke about the specific techniques by which a government in the framework of the state was able to govern people as individuals significantly useful for the world' (Foucault, 'The Political Technology of Individuals', p. 410). Thus, the police that Foucault is talking about in these lectures and in related material is an administrative agency which, through the use of extensive regulations and decrees, aimed to ensure not just adherence to the law, but also: public order; hygiene and public health; social, physical, moral and religious well-being; economic and material prosperity; and so forth. Thus, the texts that Foucault is studying as texts of the police, or texts about the doctrine of the police, are modern forms of public policy or social administration. The term 'police' is used quite early

in Foucault's work (it appears, for example, in his *History of Madness*) but he only really develops his reflections on it in the late work discussed here. For an early reference, see Michel Foucault, *History of Madness*, trans. Jonathan Murphy and Jean Khalfa (Abingdon: Routledge, 2006), p. 49.

106 See Ben Golder, 'Foucault and the Genealogy of Pastoral Power' (2007) 10 *Radical Philosophy Review* 157.

107 Foucault, *Security, Territory, Population*, pp. 125–30.

108 *Ibid.*, p. 181.

109 *Ibid.*, p. 183.

110 *Ibid.*, p. 183.

111 Foucault, 'The Subject and Power', p. 334.

112 Foucault, *Security, Territory, Population*, pp. 115–90.

113 Foucault, 'Governmentality', p. 89. This formulation does not appear in the recent translation but we retain it here because it best expresses the difference between the Machiavellian and anti-Machiavellian literatures.

114 Foucault, *Security, Territory, Population*, p. 74.

115 *Ibid.*, p. 96.

116 *Ibid.*, p. 96.

117 See Foucault, *The History of Sexuality, Vol. 1*, pp. 135–59; Foucault, *'Society Must Be Defended'*, pp. 239–63.

118 See Michel Foucault, 'Technologies of the Self', in *Essential Works of Foucault, Vol. 1: Ethics*, pp. 223–51.

119 Apart from the references in note 117, above, Foucault does not fully thematize the notion of bio-power in his work. We would argue that this is because the concept is a relatively broad one, and that (*contra* Timothy O'Leary, who argues that bio-power is 'conceptually ... included in the concept of governmentality') Foucault went in search of more historically and socially refined categories, of which governmentality and apparatuses of security represent the first examples. See Timothy O'Leary, *Foucault: The Art of Ethics* (London: Continuum, 2002), p. 178.

120 Foucault, *Security, Territory, Population*, p. 109.

121 In the years after the publication of *Discipline and Punish* Foucault was heavily criticized, primarily by the Marxist Left, for the fact that his theorization of power relations as radically dispersed and as 'capillary' failed to take adequate account of more large-scale aggregations of power (of course, the criticism was not only made by Marxists – for a feminist-inspired criticism of Foucault on this point, see Zillah R. Eisenstein, *The Female Body and the Law* (Berkeley, CA: University of California Press, 1988), pp. 16–20). Specifically, it was argued that a proper consideration of the state apparatus and the state's organization and centralization of violence was conspicuously absent from Foucault's analysis (for example, see Poulantzas, *State, Power, Socialism*, p. 44). Hence we see Foucault in this period attempt to justify and explain himself in interviews. He says, for example, that: 'I don't claim at all that the State apparatus is unimportant', and 'I don't want to say that the State isn't important; what I want to say is that relations of power, and hence the analysis that must be made of them, necessarily extend beyond the limits of the State' (Foucault, 'Body/Power', p. 60; Foucault, 'Truth and Power', p. 122). Colin Gordon reads *Security, Territory, Population* as in part a reply to Foucault's critics on this score, and he is clearly right. On this, see Colin Gordon, 'Governmental Rationality: An Introduction', in *The Foucault Effect*,

pp. 1–51 (p. 4). However, Foucault does not simply insert the state into his previous analyses of power. Rather, what Foucault proposes to do in *Security, Territory, Population* is to write neither a history nor a genealogy of the state *per se*. Rather, what he does is to resituate this object called 'the state' within the field of a practice called governmentality: 'What I would like to show you, and will try to show you, is how the emergence of the state as a fundamental political issue can in fact be situated within a more general history of governmentality, or, if you like, in the field of practices of power. ... Is it not precisely those who talk of the state, of its history, development, and claims, who elaborate on an entity through history and who develop the ontology of this thing that would be the state? What if the state were nothing more than a way of governing? What if the state were nothing more than a type of governmentality? What if all these relations of power that gradually take shape on the basis of multiple and very diverse processes which gradually coagulate and form an effect, what if these practices of government were precisely the basis on which the state was constituted?' (Foucault, *Security, Territory, Population*, pp. 247–48). Two points are immediately apparent from the foregoing. First, for Foucault the idea of governmentality is not limited to the actions of state instrumentalities – governmentalities can be operative in, and put into operation by, multiple sites and actors throughout the social body (in the family, in social groups, in workplaces, and so forth). We say 'not limited to' because of course this includes the state, and indeed the old forms of sovereignty are brought conspicuously to bear in the service of governmentality. As Foucault observes, '[t]he problem of sovereignty is not eliminated; on the contrary, it is made more acute than ever' (Foucault, *Security, Territory, Population*, p. 107). Second, for Foucault the priority is to be accorded not to 'the state' but rather to governmentality. Consequently, the more important set of questions for Foucault could well be rendered not as 'what is the state and how does it function?' but rather as, for example, 'what modalities of government are operative at a given point in time, and how do they work?'

122 Foucault, *Security, Territory, Population*, pp. 108–09.

123 *Ibid.*, pp. 107–08. Indeed, whilst Foucault is commonly read as making historical distinctions between different modalities of power which are distinctly characteristic of their time (and not without justification – see *The History of Sexuality, Vol. 1*, p. 144), he just as often observes the propinquity, co-existence and mutual interrelation of the different modalities of power. See for example his discussion of the 'scientifico-legal complex' and the '"epistemologico-juridical" formation' in *Discipline and Punish*, p. 23. As we demonstrate in the next two chapters, an epochal distinction between a sovereign-legal power that deals death and a disciplinary-bio-political power that fosters life is not only contradicted by the stubborn persistence of law itself, but also by the salient fact that for Foucault law and sovereign power cannot simply subsist in a determinate denial of life but must be ever responsive to that life and its expression.

124 Rose and Valverde, 'Governed by Law?', pp. 542–43. See also Barbara Hudson, 'Punishment and Governance' (1998) 7 *Social & Legal Studies* 553.

125 Marianne Constable, 'Sovereignty and Governmentality in Modern American Immigration Law' (1993) 13 *Studies in Law, Politics, and Society* 249, 253.

126 Foucault, *Security, Territory, Population*, p. 99 (our emphasis).

127 Kevin Walby, 'Contributions to a Post-Sovereigntist Understanding of Law: Foucault, Law as Governance, and Legal Pluralism' (2007) 16 *Social & Legal Studies* 551, 559: 'It is also crucial not to lose sight of the specificity of law by locating it in a wider field of regulation.'

128 There has been some interesting work conducted by Pat O'Malley in particular on the way in which law functions in the field of governmentality. See, for example: Pat O'Malley, 'Uncertain Subjects: Risk, Liberalism and Contract' (2000) 29 *Economy and Society* 460; Pat O'Malley, 'Imagining Insurance: Risk, Thrift and Industrial Life Insurance in Britain' (1999) 5 *Connecticut Insurance Law Journal* 675.

129 Foucault, *The History of Sexuality, Vol. 1*, p. 144.

130 In the last chapter of the first volume of *The History of Sexuality*, Foucault discusses the historical development of what he calls the sovereign right to 'decide life and death' (*ibid.*, p. 135). Such a power, for Foucault, originally inhered in the Roman father's *patria potestas*, which, Foucault asserts, permitted him to 'dispose' of the life of his children and slaves. Foucault argues that an attenuated version of this right to dispose of life (through exercising the power of death) was present in the writings of the 'classical theoreticians' who contended that the sovereign had the right to kill if he was threatened or if his laws were transgressed (p. 135). Foucault's argument is that this form of power was in fact merely the right 'to *take* life or *let* live' (p. 136, emphasis in original), and as such was limited in that it had no facility for engendering, fostering, measuring and constantly regulating life. It was against this old right of death that Foucault constructed his concept of bio-power, a power to '*foster* life or *disallow* it to the point of death' (p. 138, emphasis in original).

131 François Ewald, 'Norms, Discipline, and the Law', trans. Marjorie Beale, in *Law and the Order of Culture*, ed. Robert Post (Berkeley, CA: University of California Press, 1991), pp. 138–61 (p. 138).

132 *Ibid.*, p. 138 (emphasis in original). All internal quotations in the above quotation from Ewald's text are taken from Foucault, *The History of Sexuality, Vol. 1*, p. 144.

133 Ewald, 'Norms, Discipline, and the Law', p. 138. We have already discussed, in the text above accompanying notes 11 and 12, Foucault's notion of a juridico-discursive conception of power.

134 *Ibid.*, p. 159.

135 Foucault, *The History of Sexuality, Vol. 1*, p. 144. Although it should be remembered that Foucault consistently counterposed a legal sense of the word 'norm' to his usage in the context of disciplinary power (see note 43 above).

136 *Ibid.*, p. 89.

137 For a related reading, critical of Foucault's distinction between a constraining juridical power and a productive disciplinary one, see Judith Butler, 'Sexual Inversions', in *Foucault and the Critique of Institutions*, ed. John Caputo and Mark Yount (University Park, PA: Pennsylvania State University Press, 1993), pp. 81–98 (pp. 86–87). Butler argues that the Foucaultian distinction is a false one and that in fact the juridical is '*already productive* power, forming the very object that will be suitable for control and then, in an act that effectively disavows that production, claiming to discover that [object] outside of power' (p. 87, emphasis in original). Butler's conceptualization is indeed useful for theorizing law. Law can accordingly be seen as both productive

of *objects of control* (recall Foucault's description of discourses 'as practices that systematically form the objects of which they speak', in Michel Foucault, *The Archaeology of Knowledge*, trans. A. M. Sheridan Smith (London: Routledge, 1972), p. 49) and *subject positions*. Indeed, *The Archaeology of Knowledge* furnishes several examples of law (as discourse) constituting objects of control and subject positions (for example, see the discussion of: 'objects that are differentiated in daily practice, in law, in religious casuistry, in medical diagnosis … ' (p. 33); 'law and penal law in particular' as discourses which alongside medicine 'delimited, designated, named, and established madness as an object' (p. 42); and, finally, how law 'statutorily define[s]' the medical expert (p. 51)). See also our discussion of law's (productive) relationship to psychiatric power discussed in the text accompanying notes 87–88, above.

138 Victor Tadros, 'Between Governance and Discipline: The Law and Michel Foucault' (1998) 18 *Oxford Journal of Legal Studies* 75, 81. And on this, see Foucault, *'Society Must Be Defended'*, p. 34.

139 Tadros, 'Between Governance and Discipline', p. 82.

140 For example, see Vanessa Munro, 'Legal Feminism and Foucault – A Critique of the Expulsion of Law' (2001) 28 *Journal of Law and Society* 546; Annie Bunting, 'Feminism, Foucault, and Law as Power/Knowledge' (1992) 30 *Alberta Law Review* 829 (which does not expressly invoke Ewald but in places advances a similar argument). For Smart's arguments concerning Foucault and law, see Carol Smart, *Feminism and the Power of Law* (London: Routledge, 1989), pp. 6–9.

141 For example, see Rose and Valverde, 'Governed by Law?', p. 542; Hudson, 'Punishment and Governance', pp. 554–55.

142 Besides those quotations already discussed, and which we will return to in the next chapter, where Foucault emphasizes not the similarity or (in Ewald's account) the identity of law and norm, but rather their mutual opposition, Foucault also stated in 'The Political Technology of Individuals', that '[l]aw, by definition, is always referred to a juridical system' (p. 417). If law is *by definition* referred to a juridical system then it seems difficult to sustain an argument separating the two.

143 François Ewald, 'A Concept of Social Law', trans. Iain Fraser, in *Dilemmas of Law in the Welfare State*, ed. Gunther Teubner (New York and Berlin: Walter de Gruyter, 1988), pp. 40–75; François Ewald, 'The Law of Law', trans. Iain Fraser, in *Autopoietic Law: A New Approach to Law and Society*, ed. Gunther Teubner (New York and Berlin: Walter de Gruyter, 1988), pp. 36–50; François Ewald, 'Justice, Equality, Judgement: On "Social Justice"', trans. Iain Fraser, in *Juridification of Social Spheres: A Comparative Analysis in the Areas of Labor, Corporate, Antitrust and Social Welfare Law*, ed. Gunther Teubner (New York and Berlin: Walter de Gruyter, 1987), pp. 91–110.

144 Ewald, 'A Concept of Social Law', p. 40.

145 *Ibid.*, p. 40

146 *Ibid.*, p. 46.

147 *Ibid.*, p. 68 (emphasis in original).

148 *Ibid.*, p. 71. The internal quotation in the text from Ewald is to Michel Foucault, *La volonté de savoir* (Paris: Gallimard, 1976), p. 189.

149 Foucault, *'Society Must Be Defended'*, pp. 38–39.

150 Ivison, 'The Technical and the Political', p. 562. The internal quotations are taken from Rose and Valverde, 'Governed by Law?', p. 544.

Chapter 2

Foucault's other law

> I dream of the intellectual destroyer of evidence and universalities, the one who, in the inertias and constraints of the present, locates and marks the weak points, the openings, the lines of power, who incessantly displaces himself, doesn't know exactly where he is heading nor what he'll think tomorrow because he is too attentive to the present.[1]

When last sighted at the end of our first chapter, Foucault's law began to assume somewhat protean characteristics. Far from being simply the blunt tool of a sovereign, or the pliable instrument of disciplinary power, this law, we intimated, could well be something more. It is that ineluctable something more which we want to foreground in the present chapter. Crucially, we want to show how the movement of Foucault's law, that shifting of positions from the determinate to the beyond, from a confined law to a surpassing law which incessantly displaces itself, actually corresponds to an identifiable 'logic' of the law, itself. This necessary *ir*resolution is the constitution of the (dis)unity of Foucault's law. Thus, what we set out to do in this chapter is to derive a certain coherence from the series of apparently contradictory statements by Foucault on law. We shall revisit statements encountered in the previous chapter as well as engaging with several other texts by Foucault. In so doing, we aim to show that the seemingly opposed attributes of modern law which we shall find in Foucault's texts – the fixed and determinate law and the illimitably responsive and incipiently pervasive law; the law that is instrumentally subordinated and the surpassing law that ever eludes total control by any power – are in fact integrally related dimensions of the very same law, fractured and *ir*resolute though it seems at first to be.

In contrast to previous interpretations, our orienting concern through-out what follows is to elucidate the responsive, self-resistant dimension of Foucault's law. However, in the interests of linking our interpretation to approaches discussed in the previous chapter, we aim also to show how in law's necessarily holding itself open to, and in its becoming receptive of, that which comes or is brought to its determinate position, law is indeed – in line with the 'expulsion thesis' canvassed in Chapter 1 – susceptible to domination by ostensibly predominant powers (be they of the sovereign, the disciplinary or the bio-political variety). Where we depart from this thesis, though, is in our demonstrating how Foucault's law – not *despite* but *because of* this innate susceptibility – cannot be contained by power. Foucault's law, like his more famous (re) thinking of power as relational, cannot be rendered in any enduring stasis but, rather, must always remain incipiently responsive to the advent of alterity, and to the ineradicable and importunate demands of resistance and transgression. As we shall see, it is the impelling force of such resistance which is itself formative of Foucault's law. Indeed, in the course of the present discussion what we would most seek to show is a certain ethic of *self-resistant legality* at play in Foucault's law; not a positive core or requirement, but a restlessness which opens law to its always being otherwise.

In elaborating our reading of this Foucaultian conception of law, we rely upon many of Foucault's well known genealogical texts of the mid- to late 1970s that we discussed in Chapter 1. In addition, however, we consult a number of other important texts that are much less commonly relied upon in the literature on Foucault and law, such as, crucially, 'Maurice Blanchot: The Thought from Outside' (Foucault's 1966 engagement with the work of Maurice Blanchot) and 'A Preface to Transgression' (Foucault's 1963 homage to Georges Bataille).[2] It is in these works that the responsive dimension of Foucault's law, and its constitutive relation to the determinate dimension, begin to emerge more explicitly. And to risk repetition at this early stage, we shall argue in the course of the present chapter that Foucault's law is *both* the determined creature of orthodox accounts *and* the ever-responsive law which is constantly in excess of its determinate self – and necessarily so. It is *necessarily* so because the *ir*resolution that we perceive as being within Foucault's law is, in itself, a kind of resolution (hence, '*ir*resolution'). This *ir*resolution, we shall come to see in this chapter, is in fact the moving structure of a certain kind of unity.

We start, however, by briefly returning to matters discussed in the last chapter in order to orient our discussion. In the last chapter we intro-duced the predominant interpretation of Foucault's stance on law. This interpretation of Foucault, as we observed at the time, is hardly bereft of textual support in his writings – indeed, as we pointed out in sketching the terms of the 'expulsion thesis', our re-reading of this interpretation is not intended to undermine this position. Rather, we are trying to supplement it critically and thence to extend it. This 'expulsion thesis' essentially comprised two claims: first, that according to Foucault the law was of much less importance in modernity and that other modalities of power were coming to perform the functions (of social control, discipline, and so forth) that law used to perform in pre-modern times; and, second, that with the emergence of these new disciplinary, biopolitical or governmental modalities of power, the law was not merely surpassed, nor was it simply usurped, but it was in fact co-opted and instrumentally subordinated to the demands of these powers. In this second claim, Foucault's law is seen as being nothing but the tool of a pre-eminent power outside it – that is, law is instrumentally reduced in its relation to power. Whilst this latter claim is most often made in regard to Foucault's depictions of modernity, in which it is alleged that Foucault simply positions law as the 'rubber stamp that sanctions the functioning of [the] disciplinary system',[3] we also saw in the last chapter how Foucault at points makes law the instrument of a sovereign or monarchical administration in pre-modernity. To summarize, then, we can see that in both claims – the claim about law's becoming increasingly marginal in modernity and the claim about law's abject instrumentality – Foucault is criticized for minimizing the role of law. We can see, too, that the view of law attributed to Foucault on this reading is a contained one – such 'authorit[y] of delimitation'[4] simply 'is' the instrument of a sovereign or of disciplinary power, and nothing else. There is no possibility of its being otherwise, of its exceeding the economy of order, calculation and control to which it is assigned by power. The various efforts we examined to rehabilitate the law in Foucault's texts – whether those efforts consisted in maintaining law's co-existence with disciplinary power, or in stressing its integration with governmentality, or in arguing for its conceptual distinction from the figure of 'the juridical', for example – tended themselves to confine the law in ways not entirely dissimilar to the 'expulsion thesis'. It is against this very containment of Foucault's law, against the very possibility of its being effectively contained in any way, that our re-reading in this book is directed.

In the next section, 'Law in relation', we begin our exploration of Foucault's law by reflecting upon an aspect of the interpretations of Foucault discussed towards the end of the last chapter – namely, the argument that law exists alongside, and relates in some way to, disciplinary power. We aim to refine this argument somewhat and, in the process, to refine our understanding of Foucault's law in its relation to entities apart from it. The insistence on the part of some authors we discussed towards the end of the last chapter that Foucault did not subordinate the law to disciplinary power or governmentality and that in fact the law continued to operate alongside these power formations is a salutary reminder of the persistence of law in Foucault's account of modernity. However, here we want to develop the insight that law does not simply function in tandem with power formations such as disciplinary power, but that it in fact exists in a more complex dynamic of relation with such formations. In the second section, 'Foucault's law', we articulate a fuller picture of Foucault's law 'itself', in its opposed yet integrally related dimensions. Our focus in doing so will be the productive *ir*resolution between a present determinacy and an illimitable responsiveness to what lies beyond it. So, our argument in this chapter proceeds in two stages. First, we examine the relationship between law and disciplinary power in the section entitled 'Law in relation' in order to rebut claims that the latter surpasses and expels the former. We argue that the complicated and supplementary relation that Foucault describes between the two modalities of power reveals that law cannot simply be subordinated to disciplinary power as is claimed by proponents of the 'expulsion thesis', and that, on the contrary, disciplinary power is constituently dependent upon law. Second, in the section entitled 'Foucault's law', we focus in much greater detail upon Foucault's notion of law itself as we begin not simply to reverse the 'expulsion thesis' but to extend it by starting to articulate a more nuanced conception of Foucault's law. In our conception of Foucault's law, law is not simply rendered in terms of determinacy and closure. Rather, law can be seen to engage responsively with exteriority, with an outside made up of resistances and transgressions that assume a constituent role in law's very formation.

LAW IN RELATION

It might be simplest to start by acknowledging our ready agreement with those critics of the 'expulsion thesis' who argue that Foucault did *not* imply that the law would become diminished once we moderns had crossed the supposedly chasmic threshold separating pre-modern legality from modernity's normalizing disciplinarity. Although, as we have seen, Foucault offers several historical formulations which would tend to confirm law's being diminished – perhaps most notably where he writes of modernity as being a period of 'juridical regression'[5] – he is explicit in other places that he did not thereby 'mean to say that the law fades into the background or that the institutions of justice tend to disappear'.[6] Indeed, it is no doubt more accurate to observe that although in places

Foucault does make epochal generalizations of law's diminishing, he does frequently attempt to qualify such statements by importing some degree of nuance, historical overlap, or complication. As Ann Laura Stoler remarks, '[o]ne could read Foucault as a master at the art of crafting bold dichotomies that he recants as quickly as he sets them up'.[7] For example, in the first volume of *The History of Sexuality*, one of the ways in which Foucault frames the transition to modernity is in terms of the historical movement from a 'society of blood' to a 'society of "sex," or rather a society "with a sexuality"'.[8] The former was characterized by juridical systems of alliance and the maintenance of ties of blood and lines of descent, whilst the latter was typified by forms of power addressed to sexuality, and to the body:

> The new procedures of power that were devised during the classical age and employed in the nineteenth century were what caused our societies to go from *a symbolics of blood* to *an analytics of sexuality*. Clearly, nothing was more on the side of the law, death, transgression, the symbolic, and sovereignty than blood; just as sexuality was on the side of the norm, knowledge, life, meaning, the disciplines, and regulations.[9]

This abrupt historical distinction then receives the following qualification on the adjoining page:

> While it is true that the analytics of sexuality and the symbolics of blood were grounded at first in two very distinct regimes of power, in actual fact the passage from one to the other did not come about (any more than did these powers themselves) without overlappings, interactions, and echoes.[10]

So, recalling also Foucault's discussion of a 'triangle' of 'sovereignty, discipline, and governmental management' in the 'Governmentality' lecture that we discussed in the last chapter,[11] it is perhaps safest to assume that despite his insistence on decisive, epochal breaks,[12] Foucault can also be understood as acknowledging that matters are more intriguingly nuanced and that the different modalities of power he has described do in fact subsist together and relate in some way. As George Pavlich pithily observes, these different modalities of power are 'deployed coterminously, and in complex contextual amalgams'.[13]

We might also note that, in addition to the tendency just noted for Foucault to establish a 'bold dichotomy' only to refine it subsequently, many of his explicit statements on law itself clearly contradict his having allegedly expelled it. This is evident not only in Foucault's emphasizing that law does not fade away in modernity,[14] but also – perhaps somewhat counter-intuitively at first blush – in his repeated injunctions to 'break free … of the theoretical privilege of law and sovereignty' or to 'discover principles for analyzing power which do not derive from the system of right and the form of law'.[15] These latter comments are frequently taken by commentators on Foucault to be evidence of his desire to have done with law, indeed even to marginalize and expel it.[16] As indications that Foucault was attempting to locate new theoretical perspectives for the study of power in society, or, more precisely, to fashion a 'grid of historical decipherment'[17] for power that did not derive from law, these statements are no doubt entirely apposite. What the statements fail to demonstrate is that Foucault believed law had actually been superseded in modernity – or could ever totally be superseded – by the powers he was coming to describe. Rather, they demonstrate the contrary. As with his well known and related call to 'cut off the head of the king' in the context of contemporary political thought and analysis,[18] such pronouncements are nothing if not observations that the head of the king (and, we might also say, his various sovereign avatars in modernity) remains stubbornly attached to the rest of his body. Indeed, Foucault's insistent calls for the discovery of new theoretical principles and the metaphorical decapitation of old ones derive their force precisely from the fact that that which must supposedly be surpassed persists. Accordingly, we must be careful not to mistake Foucault's calls for renewed perspectives (even where these calls are framed in terms which would seemingly disclose an antipathy towards a certain dimension of law or right) with an observation that the law has actually been, or is in the process of being, superseded by other powers. Bearing in mind that for Foucault law and sovereignty subsisted in an integral relation, one he rendered in hyphenated propinquity as a 'system of Law-and-Sovereign',[19] we can see how this question of sovereignty's persistence also implies the persistence of law. As Foucault remarked in discussing the relation between sovereignty and governmentality, 'the problem of sovereignty was never more sharply posed' than in the eighteenth century with the transition from an art of government to a political science.[20] '[S]overeignty,' Foucault writes, 'is absolutely not eliminated by the emergence of a new art of government that has crossed the threshold of a political science. The problem of sovereignty is not eliminated; on the contrary, it is made more acute than ever.'[21] And law, too, we are told elsewhere, remains very much 'part of the social game in a society like ours'.[22] If the new powers of modernity 'effect a suspension of the law', this suspension, whilst being 'never annulled', is by the same token 'never total' either.[23] In sum, sovereignty and law persist in Foucault's modernity.

So, if Foucault frequently corrects his own historical periodizations and if many of his comments on law and on sovereignty indicate that they are still very much a central feature of modernity, then how can we understand the law's relation to the other powers that Foucault's work brings into relief? How might we, for example, understand with Nikolas Rose and Mariana Valverde the continuing 'mutual inter-dependence of law and norm',[24] or perhaps, as Anthony Beck would have it, the way in which 'modern order and power is [sic] comprised of the two systems of state-law on the one hand and the disciplines on the other'?[25] Indeed, in this last formulation, Beck echoes Foucault's own insistence that '[i]n modern societies, power is exercised through, on the basis of, and in the very play of the heterogeneity between a public right of sovereignty and a polymorphous mechanics of discipline'.[26] Is the co-existence of the law and disciplinary or bio-political power simply a question of the law working with these other powers to further its effect, to secure itself a greater penetration into the social body? Is it a question of disciplinary power operating to maximize the reach of the supposedly antique forms of legality by 'serving as an intermediary between them, linking them together, extending them and above all making it possible to bring the effects of power to the most minute and distant elements'?[27] We are clearly very far by now from the conventional view of Foucault in which he is supposed to have expelled the law – indeed, far from the law being marginalized it seems from these quotations that the law is at least of equal, if not more, importance than other forms of power in modernity such as disciplinary power and bio-power. In the following discussion we hope to refine the intimations of interdependence contained in the above formulations. These formulations are no doubt useful in that they indicate to us the persistence of law and its continued existence alongside regimes of disciplinary power, bio-power, governmentality, and so forth. However, the relation between the law and the powers that exist outside of it (and yet which repeatedly come to be inscribed within it) is, in Foucault's account, both more nuanced and more complicated than simply a question of two institutions or modalities of power operating together or alongside each other to achieve a shared goal or purpose. These statements of how the law and disciplinary power interact give the reader the impression that the law and discipline, or the law and the new administrative techniques of bio-power, are fully formed modalities which come together to work in tandem, as it were, whereas the dynamic that we want to extract from Foucault, and the theme that we want to emphasize throughout our discussion in this section, is the way in which the law and the powers supposedly external to it take identity in and through their seeming opposition to each other. It is, as Foucault would have it in a different context, in their 'existing for each other, in relation to each other, in the exchange that separates them'[28] that the unstable coherence of law (and of disciplinary power) is ceaselessly reiterated. It is the lineaments of that exchange and separation that we now want to sketch.

In charting the relationship between law and the powers that lie outside it, the first thing we can observe is that Foucault's law is frequently attached to something else. It seems never to exist in any degree of self-sustaining coherence or inviolability. In *Discipline and Punish*, often advanced as one of the ur-texts of law's expulsion in Foucault's writings, we find the law by no means expelled but, rather, constituently attached to a whole range of different entities, bodies of knowledge, or modalities of power. For example, the assertion of guilt in the 'legal machinery' is made pursuant to a whole 'scientifico-juridical complex'.[29] Indeed, Foucault's enterprise in writing *Discipline and Punish* is, he tells us very early on, to write a 'genealogy of the present scientifico-legal complex from which the power to punish derives its bases, justifications and rules'.[30] Emphasizing the importance in this endeavour of studying the role of knowledge formation and its nexus to institutional practices (perhaps more pithily encapsulated in Foucault's oft-cited formulation of 'power-knowledge'),[31] Foucault says that one of the 'four general rules' that his study will obey is the injunction to trace the history of penal law and the history of the human sciences not 'as two separate series' but rather as 'some common matrix' or, more pointedly, as 'a single process of "epistemologico-juridical" formation'.[32] Elsewhere in the same text we see that 'the whole history of modern penality' functions according to a 'juridico-anthropological' logic.[33] The law, which in certain positivist accounts is rendered in autonomous and hermetically sealed terms,[34] is here described by Foucault in relational terms. The law (or 'the juridical' in the above examples) is not so much the putatively contained entity that we have come to expect from these positivist accounts; rather, the condition of law is that of a perpetual hyphenation, reliant in some measure upon 'the scientific', 'the epistemological', and 'the anthropological' to give it some purchase (and yet it is not entirely subordinate to them, either, for as we shall see, the human sciences are themselves dependent upon law for cohering). But there are more hyphenated aspirants for the partner of law in *Discipline and Punish* besides 'the scientific', 'the epistemological', and 'the anthropological' – 'the political' also figures significantly in this relation. Indeed, Foucault's object of study in *Discipline and Punish* could well be defined as the very 'juridico-political structures of a society',[35] its 'politico-juridical model'.[36] A fuller accounting of Foucault's work would belabour a point by now, we hope, sufficiently made – that is, simply, that Foucault's law is anything but a law unto itself. Rather, in his understanding, the law and the powers apart from it would seem to be relationally inter-dependent.

To repeat, then, the theme that we have been trying to articulate here is not simply one of law's dependence upon powers and knowledges apart from it (rather, the contrary will soon emerge). In demonstrating as we have done in this section that law appears in relation to other modalities of power in Foucault's account, we have obviously disrupted any notion that law is complete, coherent and fully present to itself. However, our argument should not be taken to imply that disciplinary power and bio-power are therefore somehow confirmed in their replete self-sufficiency. Rather, our principal object in this section is to demonstrate the necessary relationship that exists between law and power (here, disciplinary power). In so doing, we aim to show how the claims made by the various commentators whom we discussed in the previous chapter, claims that disciplinary power and bio-power surpass and expel the law in Foucault's descriptive theses on modernity, are deficient precisely because they fail to address the many ways in which these techniques of power are themselves constitutively dependent upon law. In the following discussion we focus upon Foucault's concept of disciplinary power and his arguments about discipline and law (particularly as they relate to the example of the prison) in *Discipline and Punish*. We focus upon this text because it is the one most commonly relied upon by those who allege Foucault marginalized or expelled law from modernity. The dynamic that we now want to go on to instance is the dynamic of the reciprocal constitution of law and disciplinary power. The two particular examples that we draw upon in order to illustrate this dynamic reflect two related aspects of the disciplinary project: first, the making of knowledge claims about the disciplined subject through the medium of the human sciences; and, second, the response of disciplinary power to an ultimately recalcitrant subject. In our first example, we shall demonstrate how disciplinary power, in its reliance upon the knowledge claims of the human sciences, is actually dependent upon the law for its very constitution. In our second example, we shall see how law is ultimately required to respond to, and to make enforceable determinations about, the recalcitrant subject of discipline. So, reversing Foucault's terminological order of priority, we first discuss discipline's *knowledge* before concluding with discipline's *power* to punish, demonstrating in both cases that discipline must make constituent resort to law.

Let us start, then, with the link that Foucault draws between the human sciences and disciplinary power. In *Discipline and Punish* Foucault sets out to trace the rise of the human sciences through their constitutive relation to the disciplinary modality of power. While denying a simple causal link between the human sciences and the disciplinary project of, for example, the prison ('I am not saying that the human sciences emerged from the prison'),[37] Foucault nevertheless observes that if one is searching for the historical conditions of the emergence of the human sciences then:

> [o]ne should look into these procedures of writing and registration, one should look into the mechanisms of examination, into the formation of the mechanisms of discipline, and of a new type of power over bodies.[38]

Indeed:

> All the sciences, analyses or practices employing the root 'psycho-' have their origin in this reversal of the procedures of individualization. The moment that saw the transition from historico-ritual mechanisms for the formation of individuality to the scientifico-disciplinary mechanisms, when the normal took over from the ancestral, and measurement from status, thus substituting for the individuality of the memorable man that of the calculable man, that moment when the sciences of man became possible is the moment when a new technology of power and a new political anatomy of the body were implemented.[39]

Foucault hence does not argue that the human sciences simply arose out of the exigencies of the disciplinary project. Rather, his contention is that the emergence of the human sciences as a form of knowledge of 'man' is intricately linked to the emergence of the new 'technology of power', or 'new political anatomy of the body', that was taking shape at the turn of the eighteenth century.[40] And indeed the prison (as well as the asylum, the workhouse, the school, and so forth) was a crucial site for the generation of disciplinary knowledge, a knowledge which thenceforth came to be generalized throughout the social body. For our purposes here, however, it is simply important to note that the assured functioning of disciplinary power is dependent upon the production of scientific knowledges of 'man' – these are the 'scientifico-disciplinary mechanisms' that Foucault refers to in the above quotations from *Discipline and Punish*.[41] The finite calculability of 'man', his rendering in tables, case files, documentary records and examination reports, is essential to disciplinary power's modulation of time and space, and its insistent control of the human body. Disciplinary power is constitutively linked to the knowledge of the individual and society and the way in which the 'reversal of the procedures of individualization'[42] rendered necessary the giving of every person (not just the politically powerful or the socially significant) a distinct individuality, a discrete place in the great social continuum of abnormal to normal. As Foucault observes, writing of the linkage between the truth-effects of the human sciences and disciplinary power, 'we are judged, condemned, forced to perform tasks, and destined to live and die in certain ways by discourses that are true, and which bring with them specific power-effects'.[43]

Yet this politically useful scientific knowledge, as Foucault's analyses reveal, is a fractured and incomplete one. The claim of this knowledge in its own terms to 'scientific' and 'true' status is never entirely and convincingly made out.[44] Lacking a transcendent reference point in modernity, the human sciences are called upon to speak the truth of society to itself from an entirely immanent position – one which aims to secure a comprehension of the social field from a position within that field itself. Yet with no compendious position apart from society from which the truth of the whole, indeed even the truth of the individual in his or her very being, can be definitively known, this demonstrative task is rendered impossible and the presumptuous epistemological project to know the essence of the individual and society is necessarily rendered incomplete (which is not to deny the quality of the faith expressed in the human sciences, in and through their very incompletion, to go beyond the demonstrated and reveal ever more truth). If, then, disciplinary power's knowledge is ultimately lacking in its epistemological reach and in its extravagant claims to encompass a totality, what agency can help to (re)constitute disciplinary power and the failed discourse of the human sciences? The answer, or at any rate one of the answers, Foucault tells us, is law.

In *Discipline and Punish*, Foucault writes of the way in which the law acts to provide compensatory justification and authority for the incomplete epistemological project of disciplinary power and its knowledge claims about the individual and society:

> But the supervision of normality was firmly encased in a medicine or a psychiatry that provided it with a sort of 'scientificity'; it was supported by a judicial apparatus which, directly or indirectly, gave it legal justification. Thus, in the shelter of these two considerable protectors, and, indeed, acting as a link between them, or a place of

exchange, a carefully worked out technique for the supervision of norms has continued to develop right up to the present day.[45]

And again:

Carceral continuity and the fusion of the prison-form make it possible to legalize, or in any case to legitimate disciplinary power, which thus avoids any element of excess or abuse it may entail.[46]

One of the ways in which the law achieves the aim of constituting the authority of disciplinary power is – paradoxically, it might seem – to act, and to be seen to act, as a restraint upon it. In the words of one of the commentators on Foucault whom we discussed in the last chapter, we might say that it is through law's 'framing' of disciplinary power that the relationship between the two begins to emerge more clearly.[47] Again, what we want to show in the example of the prison is the way in which the law sets itself up in putative opposition to disciplinary power and, in so doing, works symbiotically with it in order both to shore up its own position as law, and to perform this constituting task for disciplinary power. How, then, does law compensate for disciplinary power's deficits? Again, the metaphor of framing, of encircling and of asserting jurisdiction, is apposite here. The jurisdictional ruse by which law asserts its own power and in the process goes to constitute disciplinary power is really quite a simple one. That is, by purporting to exercise its supervisory jurisdiction only over the more egregious aberrations, abuses and excesses of disciplinary power, law confirms the basic claim at the heart of disciplinary power to adjudicate on questions of normality and social cohesion. In so doing, it inscribes the disciplinary project in the very nature of things, 'confirming' its tenuous grasp on a scientifically comprehended and disciplinarily administered world and simply acting to correct its application in those cases where something goes amiss. Thus, in confining its legal supervision to the contested *periphery*, the instability at the very *core* of disciplinary power (the lack of epistemological certitude and authority for its normalizing project) is left unquestioned and hence reinforced. It is solely those instances of disciplinary power's application which, in the margins, appear somewhat excessive that receive the legal treatment – everything else is plausibly rendered, in the language of disciplinary power itself, normal, as the norm. Crucially, the disciplinary excesses must be diverted and accounted for by law lest they undermine the asserted coherence of the disciplinary entity itself. As we shall see later on with the example of discipline's ultimate inability to enforce itself, discipline is here constituently reliant upon law to rein in its excesses. As bare assertion of actuality, discipline lacks the ability to adapt responsively and it is reliant upon law to deal with this constitutive insufficiency. This is the gesture that the law performs for disciplinary power, and we can see it in the apt example (apt, that is, given Foucault's focal concern with the prison in *Discipline and Punish*) of the judicial review of disciplinary hearings in prisons.

We focus here upon a specific historical example – namely, a 1988 decision of the United Kingdom House of Lords, acting in its capacity as an appellate court. Our analysis of this particular case is intended to reveal something of the relational dynamic of law and disciplinary power. At issue in the case was the question of the scope of legal representation for prisoners in gaols in England and Wales charged with disciplinary offences. At the time, such hearings were generally conducted by the prison governor or by a select (external) Board of Visitors convened to adjudicate on disciplinary charges brought by the prison authorities. Whether a charge was heard by the governor or by the Board of Visitors depended upon the seriousness of the penalty (the Board of Visitors heard charges where the penalty was more serious in terms of the number of days of remission that could be forfeited by the prisoner).[48] Briefly, the specific issue joined in the case of *R v Board of Visitors of HM Prison, The Maze* ex parte *Hone*[49] was the question of whether the requirements of natural justice imported a right for an aggrieved prisoner to be represented before the Board of Visitors. Lord Goff of Chieveley's opinion neatly illustrates the deferential withdrawal of the law in its supervisory guise, and further illustrates how this withdrawal confirms the knowledge claims of disciplinary power. Lord Goff started by denying that a general right of representation existed. Rather, the provision of legal representation would have to be dependent upon the context of the particular dispute or disciplinary charge. Providing for a general right of representation in the prison system (where 'disgruntled prisoners', to use a phrase of Lord Denning's in a similar context, could make 'the governor's life ... intolerable')[50] was deemed inappropriate for a body 'exercising a disciplinary jurisdiction'.[51] That is, the carefully tailored exercise of disciplinary power at the coalface of delinquency issues could not realistically be tethered by the 'in principle' bequeathing of abstract, legal rights. As Lord Goff put it, '[t]o hold otherwise would result in wholly unnecessary delays in many cases ... and ... wholly unnecessary waste of time and money, contrary to the public interest'.[52]

Yet it is the conclusion to Lord Goff's opinion, in which he discusses how and why natural justice does not import a right to representation in hearings before the governor, that is most revealing. Here, as well as the obfuscations of inappropriateness and the intrusion of those perennial justifications of time, money and the public interest, we can observe the judicial naturalization of disciplinary power:

> The jurisdiction exercised by the Governor is of a more summary nature [than that exercised by the Board of Visitors], and should properly be exercised with great expedition. ... In the nature of things, it is difficult to imagine that the rules of natural justice would ever require legal representation before the Governor.[53]

This is not simply an endorsement of untrammelled gubernatorial expedition and the exigent dispensing of summary justice. It is, more importantly, a perfect example of the legal sanction that judicial review gives to disciplinary power. By withdrawing its legal claim to supervise, by quarantining the disciplinary scene, the law confirms disciplinary power as being simply, as Lord Goff aptly puts it, '[i]n the nature of things'.[54] This nature is not, however, pre-existing. It is an artifact of law's withdrawal and of law's self-limitation. By not attempting to rule, law carves a space in which disciplinary power does not simply operate but operates naturally and in the true order of things. Thus, the quotidian operations of prison discipline – its tabulation and hierarchical organization of offenders according to scales of behaviour and (ab)normality; its incessant production, and sanctioning, of delinquency – remain untouched by the law, but, what is more, are constituted as normal and natural operations by this very removal. And, in return, these 'scientifico-disciplinary mechanisms'[55] which isolate delinquency and abnormality give to the law a certain compensating legitimacy of its own, allowing the law to function 'on a general horizon of "truth"':

> That the grip of the prison on the penal system should not have led to a violent reaction of rejection is no doubt due to many reasons. One of these is that, in fabricating delinquency, it gave to criminal justice a unitary field of objects, authenticated by the 'sciences', and thus enabled it to function on a general horizon of 'truth'.[56]

For law, too, as Foucault writes elsewhere, 'must appear to be a necessity of things';[57] it must ultimately be 'grounded in truth'.[58] The scientificity of the disciplines hands to the law the power of this truth, although as we have just seen it is law which guarantees for discipline its 'unitary field of objects', as the above quotation from *Discipline and Punish* has it. Thus in their relation both the law and disciplinary power serve to constitute the other as natural and necessary. By submitting itself to the supervisory jurisdiction of the rule of law (however attenuated and tangential this oversight actually proves to be in practice) disciplinary power helps consolidate law's claim to rule without the law actually being called upon to make good on its promise of being able to do, and rule over, anything. And if discipline is given 'legal justification' and its actions are made 'legitimate' through the exercise of a restrained judicial supervision,[59] then, as we have seen, that same discipline allows the law to function on a certain domain of truth (we shall return later in the chapter to the question of law's operative dependence upon powers apart from it). The law, in turn, appears in this relation as a guarantee of the naturalness of that which it itself serves to constitute as natural.

Thus far we have argued that disciplinary power, in its reliance upon the knowledge claims of the human sciences, is ultimately constrained by the epistemological failure of that apparatus of knowledge. There is hence a constituent reliance by discipline upon law for its cohering. What we want to illustrate in the remainder of this section is how, passing now from the 'knowledge' to the 'power' side of Foucault's famously synoptic equation, there is still perforce a second resort made by the disciplinary to the legal. Put simply, the mere factuality of the scientific fails adequately to deal with instances of utter recalcitrance. Even with the constitutive compensations of law at the level of the human sciences, disciplinary power must further rely on law in order to deal with sheer insubordination, with the very importunacy of the undisciplined upon which its continuate being depends. This lack reveals the limit of the disciplinary project's power to punish – it is the limit at which the suasive claims of scientificity must ever give way to the enforceable determination of law. As we have argued, the demonstrative claims of the human sciences to compendiously encapsulate the truth of the individual and his or her place within a similarly contained society are necessarily incomplete. The human sciences fail to provide a definitive template of normality within which the individual and society become intelligible – for Foucault, as we shall soon see, the singularity of the recalcitrant subject ever escapes the operations of disciplinary power and the vaunted encompassments of its 'scientific' knowledge formations. What this imports for discipline is a further reliance on law – a law which through its modalities of determination and decision surpasses the merely demonstrative nature of discipline and its knowledge formations. Let us first set the (disciplinary) scene.

Law's retreat from the site of discipline, a site which law has a significant role in constituting, facilitates the workings of disciplinary power and allows it to operate largely unencumbered by juridical constraints. In the relationship between them, the institutional space inhabited by the disciplines is, as we have seen, an artifact of law's self-withdrawal, or, as Foucault puts it in '*Society Must Be Defended*', 'the organization of a juridical code ... made it possible to superimpose on the mechanism of discipline a system of right that concealed its mechanisms and erased the element of domination and the techniques of domination involved in discipline'.[60] The juridical code thus masks the domination of disciplinary power by proffering the sanctioning imprimatur of legality.[61] In the spaces left vacant by a self-limiting legality, on the very 'underside of the law' as it were,[62] disciplinary power practises its 'supervision of normality'[63] through the techniques of spatial distribution, hierarchical observation, normalizing judgment, constant surveillance, and examinations.

However, the disciplinary production of compliance is not and cannot be a univocal enterprise. Recalcitrance is not completely subdued by the demands of the dictated norm. Rather, it is both a central component of the disciplinary power relation itself and that which necessarily exceeds it. Recalcitrance is both unavoidable and indeed indispensable for the furtherance of the disciplinary project, being necessary to provoke disciplinary power into an ever more attuned existence. Yet as we shall see in the next section, 'Foucault's law', such a recalcitrant provocation constitutes more than a simple 'correction' to disciplinary power and is in fact formative of its very being, of the borders of the disciplinary norm itself.

That recalcitrance is an ever-present, immanent dimension of disciplinary power stems from the fact that the inculcation of the 'scientifically' mandated norms of discipline is dependent upon the subjects of discipline themselves. As Foucault writes in *Discipline and Punish*:

> He who is subjected to a field of visibility, and who knows it, assumes responsibility for the constraints of power; he makes them play spontaneously upon himself; he inscribes in himself the power relation in which he simultaneously plays both roles; he becomes the principle of his own subjection.[64]

And, as Foucault later obligingly reveals, there is in this relation (and more to the point there *must* be) the possibility of 'voluntary inservitude, of reflexive indocility' on the part of the disciplinary subject.[65] There is in any power relation always 'something which is by no means a more or less docile or reactive primal matter, but rather a centrifugal movement, an inverse energy, a discharge'.[66] Discipline hence fails fully to master its subject, or, in the later language of bio-power: 'It is not that life has been totally integrated into techniques that govern and administer it; it constantly escapes them.'[67] That 'escape' from a disciplinary subjectification is thematized more explicitly by Foucault in his later work on governmentality and ethics (which we discuss in greater depth in Chapter 3) as a withdrawal from attempts to encapsulate the 'truth' of the subject. The government of subjects through truth (and especially the subject's *self*-subjection to a discourse of truth about his or her being) was a central theoretical and political concern of Foucault's in this period and it is here that he emphasizes how practices of resistance to this type of 'government of individuals by their own verity'[68] can take the form of a 'desubjectification'. For Foucault, such 'desubjectification' entails a distancing, a retreating of oneself from existing modes of truth-based subjectification and from the array of politically available modes of being. As he writes, '[t]he essential function of critique would be that of desubjectification in the game of what one could call, in a word, the politics of truth'.[69]

The 'failure' of these errant subjects who assume responsibility for their own disciplinary subjection is a necessary and productive one for disciplinary power. This recalcitrance which flows from the non-encapsulation of the subject 'forms the motivation for every new development of networks of power'.[70] As Foucault's discussion of the (re)production of delinquency in *Discipline and Punish* makes clear, discipline both produces and relies upon a recalcitrant resistance to the power of the scientifically administered norm. In other words, failure is generative:

> For a century and a half the prison had always been offered as its own remedy: the reactivation of the penitentiary techniques as the only means of overcoming their perpetual failure; the realization of the corrective project as the only method of overcoming the impossibility of implementing it.[71]

Indeed, this generative recalcitrance is something Foucault later comes to see as definitive of power relations in general. As he observes in the essay, 'The Subject and Power':

> In this game, freedom may well appear as the condition for the exercise of power (at the same time its precondition, since freedom must exist for power to be exerted, and also its permanent support, since without the possibility of recalcitrance power would be equivalent to a physical determination).[72]

Yet if there is an integral and impelling reliance by disciplinary formations upon that which would resist them, upon those residual instances of recalcitrance which unceasingly and generatively form 'their limit, their underside, their counter-stroke',[73] there is nevertheless a point at which these disciplinary formations fail to deal with ultimate recalcitrance. Disciplinary power, as we have seen, relies upon the normative evaluations of the human sciences. But the human sciences cannot in and of themselves deal with a total refusal of the norm, with that which escapes it and calls for a decision. Simply put, they can identify and stigmatize abnormality but not enforce sanctions against it of their own scientific motion. For this, discipline must resort once again to a different modality – at the recalcitrant limit of discipline stands the law, a law which must be within the disciplinary scene yet also hold itself apart. Hence Foucault's repeated observations in *Discipline and Punish*, in the very same moment that he wants to maintain a conceptual space between norm and law,[74] of the legal within the disciplinary. In *Discipline and Punish* we are told, for example, that '[a]t the heart of all disciplinary systems functions a small penal mechanism ... [which] enjoys a kind of judicial privilege with its own laws, its specific offences, its particular forms of judgement'[75] and which even takes place within 'a small-scale model of the court'.[76] Indeed, as Foucault observes in the same work, '[i]n appearance, the disciplines constitute nothing more than an infra-law'.[77] Moreover, the judicial form is constantly inscribed within the disciplinary technology of power. 'We are in,' Foucault informs us, 'the society of the teacher-judge, the doctor-judge, the educator-judge, the "social worker"-judge'.[78] In showing us a disciplinary norm which stands outside or beneath a juridical law and which relies upon the force of the human sciences for its application, and a norm which has resort to the juridical in the final event of recalcitrance, Foucault is demonstrating discipline's dependence upon law. In our reading of Foucault, it is hence at the limit of generative recalcitrance that the scientificity of the observed *norm* gives way to the enforceable juridicism of the *law*.

So, all in all, the dynamic of law's relationship to disciplinary power that we have traced in this section is quite clearly not one of simple dependence, as proponents of the 'expulsion thesis' contend. To the contrary, we have tried to describe the reciprocal compensation between the power of discipline and the power of law in the very 'play of the[ir] heterogeneity',[79] a process which reveals that discipline is in fact constituently dependent upon law in the realms of both knowledge and power. Such a reliance clearly belies claims of law's expulsion. The 'communication between the power of discipline and the power of the law'[80] which Foucault describes in *Discipline and Punish* hence illustrates a relationship in which, in their integral combining, discipline and law remain mutually incomplete. Having focused in this section upon the ways in which discipline cannot be comprehensively coherent, we move in the next section to identify a generative incoherence of law. Our theme, as we indicated in our introductory remarks at the beginning of this chapter, will be the integral yet unsettled combining of the determinate and the responsive dimensions of Foucault's law.

FOUCAULT'S LAW: RESISTANCE, TRANSGRESSION, LAW

Thus far we have tried to set out our understanding of two of the ways in which law relates to disciplinary power. In the process, we have sought to show both how law is dependent upon the powers outside it and how these powers are themselves dependent upon the law. This theme of mutual constitution and relationality, in which disciplinary power is not 'under the immediate dependence or a direct extension of ... juridico-political structures ... [but is] nonetheless not absolutely independent'[81] of their influence, is one way of demonstrating how, as against the 'expulsion thesis', law does still figure prominently in Foucault's modernity. In so doing, we have tried to refine somewhat the intimations of law's continuing relevance, or perhaps simply its persistence into modernity, contained in some of the scholarship on Foucault discussed towards the end of the last chapter. However, Foucault's attitude towards the law was far more radical, and more complex, than simply an assertion that it remained in place alongside the new powers he was describing – even in the more nuanced way in which we have tried to frame matters here.

In attempting to capture something more of Foucault's law, the argument that we develop in this section is that Foucault illustrates for us two crucial dimensions of law, dimensions uneasily but integrally related. The first dimension is the one more persistently remarked upon in his work – a determinate law which expresses a definite content. This is, if you will, law 'on the side of' the norm – a law to be resisted and transgressed. The second dimension of law is that dimension in which law, in a constitutive engagement by way of that same resistance and transgression, extends itself illimitably in its attempt to encompass and respond to what lies outside its definite content. This is a law of mutability, a law which is constantly in excess of its determinate self and which is uncontainable in and by its present instantiations. Law in this responsive dimension forms itself through an encounter with its outside, with what lies beyond itself. Law thence becomes self-resistant, disrupting itself through becoming receptive of resistances that constantly challenge its position, its content, its being. In reading Foucault, we repeatedly encounter these two dimensions of law: the determinate law and the responsive law that is ever inclined beyond itself, amenably unmade by resistance. As we hope the following discussion demonstrates, however, this distinction between the determinate 'rigidity of the law'[82] and its going ever beyond this same rigidity in an incipiently pervasive responsiveness is not a distinction between two opposed understandings of law but, to use more explicitly Foucaultian terminology, two modalities of the very same law. What we shall demonstrate is that these two dimensions of law are in fact necessary dimensions of the one law, and that Foucault's law finds its unsettled 'place' in the movement between them. Indeed, as Foucault observes, '[w]hat rule could survive if it did not breathe irregularity on a daily basis?'[83] Thus, when we come to examine Foucault's law in this section we find not a wholly determinate law but rather one of just 'relative stability'.[84] Foucault's law, we shall find, is necessarily a creature of both determinacy and responsiveness. In its being thus it is ultimately – despite premature reports of its demise or instrumental reduction canvassed in Chapter 1 – an uncontrollable law, a law of resistance, a resistant law.

As a prelude to their combining, let us first discuss these different dimensions of Foucault's law in turn, starting with the more determinate manifestation. This, with admittedly ample warrant, was the view of law attributed to Foucault by many of the theorists we discussed in Chapter 1. Here we see law reduced, in its opposition to the 'unbalanced, heterogeneous, unstable, and tense force relations' of power's fecund positivity, to a matter of 'institutional crystallization'.[85] Law is simply one of the 'terminal forms' which 'power takes' – a power which is always in excess of law.[86] Law seems set in its negative mode of restraint and calculation, in its being nothing more than the 'law which says no'[87] and 'the law of prohibition'.[88] This law is characterized by 'simple and endlessly reproduced mechanisms',[89] by the very 'poverty and monotony of interdictions'.[90] Where such a stultified law is allowed some involving creative capacity, some ability to extend or reorient itself, it is unhappily confined to 'imagin[ing] the negative'.[91] Such, as the proponents of the 'expulsion thesis' would have it, seems to be Foucault's abiding view of law as negative, limited, mechanical and determinate. There is no ability for it to transcend its instant manifestations, for it to be otherwise than what it is. Foucault's law in this dimension simply represents the pursuit of certainty and predictability, the measured imposition of a determinate order upon the endlessly variegated world.[92] In this vein, Foucault tells us that the purpose of the judicial apparatus is to 'produce what has the highest values in civilizations like ours: social order',[93] or that 'order is what remains' when the work of law is accomplished.[94] As we have been hinting at in our discussion, however, this determinate securing of order is only one half of the story of Foucault's law, for there is of course another Foucault (one just as much if not more remarked) for whom such solidities could never hold. Let us now engage that other Foucault, and thus introduce the responsive dimension of Foucault's law through a discussion, first, of power and resistance, and then of transgression and the limit.

This other Foucault – a Foucault whom we briefly encountered above in our discussion of disciplinary power and recalcitrance – was the theorist of power's dispersion,[95] and of its generative reliance upon resistance. Famously, for the Foucault of the mid- to late 1970s, power could not be contained in a single centre or locus – we must not seek power, Foucault directs us, 'in the primary existence of a central point, in a unique source of sovereignty from which secondary and descendant forms would emanate'.[96] Consequently, for Foucault, neither the state nor a privileged economic class could ever be the anointed, determinate and enduring repository of power. Power was neither embodied by certain actors, nor encapsulated in any given 'institution' or 'structure'.[97] Rather, power was 'the moving substrate of force relations' immanent in the social field.[98] Power existed only in relation – a constant relation which suffused the entire social body and which was negotiated and renegotiated, produced and reproduced 'from one moment to the next'.[99] This relational conception of power was articulated against what Foucault saw as the theoretically impoverished conception of power then dominant in legal and political thinking. According to Foucault, the proponents of this 'juridico-discursive' theory of power,[100] in their constitutional, liberal political or Marxist guises, effectively reduced and constrained power. On the juridico-discursive view, power is understood either as a commodity that some political actors can determinately secure, alienate, or exercise to the detriment of others, or as a superstructural effect of relations of economic production.[101] For Foucault, however, power was neither the outcome of a contractual process, nor the cherished result of economic domination:

> Power is not something that is acquired, seized, or shared, something that one holds on to or allows to slip away; power is exercised from innumerable points, in the interplay of nonegalitarian and mobile relations.[102]

Again:

> Power must, I think, be analyzed as something that circulates, or rather as something that functions only when it is part of a chain. It

is never localized here or there, it is never in the hands of some, and it is never appropriated in the way that wealth or a commodity can be appropriated. Power functions.[103]

This power, in a famous formulation:

comes from below; that is, there is no binary and all-encompassing opposition between rulers and ruled at the root of power relations, and serving as a general matrix – no such duality extending from the top down and reacting on more and more limited groups to the very depths of the social body. One must suppose rather that the manifold relationships of force that take shape and come into play in the machinery of production, in families, limited groups, and institutions, are the basis for wide-ranging effects of cleavage that run through the social body as a whole. These then form a general line of force that traverses the local oppositions and links them together; to be sure, they also bring about redistributions, realignments, homogenizations, serial arrangements, and convergences of the force relations. Major dominations are the hegemonic effects that are sustained by all these confrontations.[104]

From the above quotations, taken from some of his representative writings of the mid- to late 1970s, a familiar Foucaultian picture of power begins to emerge. Power assumes characteristically fluid dimensions, dimensions in which it can neither be fully encompassed or defined, nor rendered in any set and enduring form. Whilst in modern disciplinary (or, latterly, bio-political) society modalities of power and political technologies can be reproduced, appropriated and redeployed, power *as such* can never be ultimately secured. That this uncontainable, somewhat ephemeral notion of power can only ever be grasped in relation has led to some predictable consternation on the part of Foucault's critics when it comes to the small matter of resistance. If Foucault tends to displace the state and other forms of structural oppression (class, patriarchy, and so forth) from their privileged positions as objects of analysis and critique in political theory, then surely this displacement attenuates the possibilities of effective resistance to precisely those agents who exercise power to most telling effect?[105] More fundamentally, perhaps, if power is, as Foucault puts it, an 'omnipresence',[106] if indeed it is 'everywhere'[107] and 'there is no outside'[108] from which to contest it, then how and from where could resistance possibly take place? Against these queries, and reversing their order of priority, we want in what follows to show the centrality of resistance – indeed even a primacy of resistance – to Foucault's notion of power. That is to say, in Foucault's resonant phrase, 'resistance comes first'.[109]

If the field of the social is invested through and through with formations of power, if indeed power is definitive of the social, nevertheless these mobile, ever-shifting power formations exist in a constituent relationship with contrary formations of resistance. 'Where there is power,' Foucault remarks, 'there is resistance.'[110] If '[p]ower is everywhere',[111] then, by the same token, 'points of resistance are present everywhere in the power network'.[112] This felicitous conjunction of power and resistance is not a simple coincidence of forces, and neither is it the case that resistance only galvanizes itself in response to power's advances. Resistances, Foucault stresses, are not a mere 'reaction or rebound, forming with respect to the basic domination an underside that is in the end always passive, doomed to perpetual defeat', they are not 'a lure or a promise that is of necessity betrayed'.[113] Rather, resistance is *constitutive* of power. The very 'existence' of power relations 'depends upon a multiplicity of points of resistance'.[114] Now, whilst Foucault does in places describe the role of resistance in rather supine terms as the 'adversary, target, support, or handle in power relations',[115] it is clear from his many other observations that he envisages a more fundamental and impelling role for resistance. Thus, if the existence of power is predicated upon resistance this is not merely because resistance supports power or provides its 'motivation'[116] but rather because power formations ultimately derive their very content, their very being, from the impelling movement of resistance. These resistances, these 'mobile and transitory points of resistance', come to 'inscribe [themselves] in [power relations] as an irreducible opposite', repeatedly contesting and reforming power throughout and across the social body.[117] '[R]esistance is never in a position of exteriority in relation to power' for the precise reason that it comes to invest and inhabit power,[118] bequeathing it content and form. As Foucault says, 'There is not, on the one side, a discourse of power, and opposite it, another discourse that runs counter to it.'[119] Such binaries 'misunderstand the strictly relational character of power relationships',[120] a relationality which imports a formative force of resistance. As Foucault remarks in a later piece, resistance resides '[a]t the very heart of the power relationship ... constantly provoking it'.[121] Any given instantiation of power is thus dependent upon formations of resistance that impel it and that, in inscribing themselves within the power relation, come to form it and give it substance.[122] Thus, reversing the standard take on resistance which would see resistance in terms of a resiling from or a responding to power, Foucault sees power itself as responsive to (and generatively formed by) resistance. Hence his insistence that we should 'tak[e] the forms of resistance against different forms of power as a starting point' for our enquiries into power relations.[123] Consequently, following this reversal of perspective, if we want to 'find out what our society means by "sanity," perhaps we should investigate what is happening in the field of insanity. And what we mean by "legality" in the field of illegality'.[124]

What arises from Foucault's reflections on the indissoluble relationship between power and resistance is hence not a perceived pervasion of unsurpassable power for which he is frequently and reductively criticized.[125] Power is not, as Foucault emphasized in a late discussion, 'an inescapable fatality at the heart of societies, such that it cannot be undermined'.[126] Instead, formations of power are constitutively lacking, always in the process of ruination and being undermined and re-formed by resistance. There is always something which 'escapes' them.[127] Foucault thus does not posit a stable and determinate instantiation of power, but rather a mobile and constantly shifting relation between power and that which contests it from outside. Any power formation, if it is to continue in force, must respond to and incorporatively engage with the 'diversity of forms and extensions, of energies and irreducibilities' of resistance,[128] for 'there has never existed one type of stable subjugation, given once and for all', that was immune from the 'effects of resistance and counterinvestments'.[129] That is to say, finally, that if 'resistance comes first' and 'resistance remains superior to [the forces of power]', then 'power relations are obliged to change with the resistance'.[130]

The relation between resistance and the formative responsiveness of regimes of power also figures in Foucault's earlier thinking on transgression from the 1960s. Whilst we do not equate the two notions of transgression and resistance here, nevertheless the mutually constitutive relationship between transgression and the limit shares a similar dynamic with Foucault's later discussions of resistance and power.[131] In 'A Preface to Transgression', Foucault's 1963 homage to the French novelist and philosopher Georges Bataille, Foucault sets out to chart the experience of a restless modern 'world exposed by the experience of its limits, made and unmade by that excess which transgresses it'.[132] In such a world: 'The play of limits and transgression seems to be regulated by a simple obstinacy: transgression incessantly crosses and recrosses a line which closes up behind it.'[133] 'But,' Foucault counsels, this relationship between an excessive, ruptural transgression and the implacable limit which it besieges 'is considerably more complex'[134] than such a simple view would allow:

> Transgression ... is not related to the limit as black to white, the prohibited to the lawful, the outside to the inside, or the open area

of a building to its enclosed spaces. Rather, their relationship takes the form of a spiral which no simple infraction can exhaust.[135]

In the result, there is a constituent reliance by the instituted limit upon that which would oppose it. Transgression itself constitutes the limit, it 'affirms limited being – affirms the limitlessness into which it leaps as it opens this zone to existence for the first time'.[136] Indeed Foucault questions whether the limit could even 'have a life of its own outside of the act that gloriously passes through it and negates it'.[137] And yet transgression, that impalpable 'flash of lightning in the night', does not stand utterly apart from the limit and on its own terms.[138] Rather it derives its very being through and in its relation to the limit, in the 'moment',[139] the 'curious intersection'[140] of its engagement with the limit. Indeed, it 'know[s] no other life'[141] outside this formative intersection. Ultimately:

> The limit and transgression depend on each other for whatever density of being they possess: a limit could not exist if it were absolutely uncrossable and, reciprocally, transgression would be pointless if it merely crossed a limit composed of illusions and shadows.[142]

We have thus seen how, for Foucault, power must constantly respond to a resistance which comes to occupy and re-form it, and how it is in the very movement of transgression composing and recomposing the limit that the world is ever 'made and unmade'.[143] And, as with power and the limit, so too, we now show, with law. For Foucault, law cannot simply exist in a determinate solidity, in the calibrated expression of a rule or the imposition of an enduring order. Rather, law must necessarily assume a labile existence, and this is what we have been calling the *responsiveness* of Foucault's law.[144] Whilst law must assume a definite content – and this content is given to law in standard jurisprudential perceptions by such entities as a sovereign, a class, a society, and so forth – the law cannot remain tied to any given content and must incorporatively engage with what is other to it, with resistances and transgressions which challenge its position.

Foucault explicitly thematizes this other dimension of law, this necessary responsiveness of law, through an engagement with the work of his contemporary, the French novelist and philosopher, Maurice Blanchot. In the context of a discussion of two of Blanchot's novels, Foucault evokes a law of mutability, a law which practises an 'infinitely accommodating welcome'[145] to what lies beyond it. Never determinately settled in any one instantiation, this law is:

the outside that envelops conduct, thereby removing it from all interiority; it is the darkness beyond its borders; it is the void that surrounds it, converting, unknown to anyone, its singularity into the gray monotony of the universal and opening around it a space of uneasiness, of dissatisfaction, of multiplied zeal.[146]

Far from being the stilled creature of determinacy and stasis, this law is constantly on the move, being 'track[ed] ... into its lair',[147] 'envelop [ing] precisely what had tried to overturn it'.[148] Foucault asks of this restless law:

How could one know the law and truly experience it, how could one force it to come into view, to exercise its powers clearly, to speak, without provoking it, without pursuing it into its recesses, without resolutely going ever farther into the outside into which it is always receding?[149]

The above quotation comes from Foucault's engagement with Blanchot, who himself observes of law that:

Law ... exists only in regard to its transgression-infraction and through the rupture that this transgression, infraction believes it produces, while the infraction only justifies, renders just what it breaks or defies.[150]

And Blanchot would add also:

Let us grant that the law is obsessed with exteriority, by that which beleaguers it and from which it separates via the very separation that institutes it as form, in the very movement by which it formulates this exteriority as law.[151]

Foucault's law, then, engages formatively with exteriority, being ever 'constrained to perpetually reach beyond itself'.[152] Like power, Foucault's law cannot be 'given once and for all',[153] but must constantly remain in negotiation with powers which, as Blanchot has it in the above quotation, 'beleaguer it' from outside. As Foucault writes elsewhere of this restive and ever-expanding law, this law which is 'resolutely' oriented towards its outside,[154] it may well be 'part of the destiny of the law to absorb little by little elements that are alien to it'.[155] And yet Foucault only hints at the range of law's responsiveness in such a formulation, for law's responsiveness to an outside cannot be pre-ordained and accounted for in advance and is not a matter of an enduring law simply absorbing and assimilating all that is foreign to it. Indeed, this receptivity of the law, this ever-opening by which the law disrupts its determinate self and by which it is incipiently attuned to 'the outside into which it is always receding',[156] can well be more in the nature of an effective occupation than an incremental absorption, to which Foucault's repeated discussions of law's being 'invaded', 'colonized', and such, aptly attest.[157] Hence of course the prevalence of observations that, for Foucault, 'the juridical values of the law are completely overwhelmed by scientific-administrative norms' and that discipline comes to instrumentally reduce law to the imperatives of its 'scientific-administrative' order.[158] However, as we shall go on to demonstrate in the following pages when we discuss the question of law's vacuity, it is in its being constitutively responsive to new content and new forms that Foucault's law ultimately eludes encapsulation by power, and hence such descriptions of law's occupation and its overwhelming by power are inaccurate. What we simply want to raise at this stage of our argument, though, is this very attunement to alterity, this capacity of Foucault's law in its responsive dimension to be otherwise than what it is.

To recap for the moment, then, Foucault illuminates two salient dimensions of modern law. As most commentators are quick to point out, Foucault offers in some places a remarkably static and bare account of law as a calculating tool of social order, a law which operates negatively to control and circumscribe. However, in our reading of Foucault, this law of determinacy is only one side of the equation of law, as it were. There is another law, or at any rate another dimension or mode of becoming of the law, which we have been calling law's responsiveness. In this dimension, law extends itself, constantly opening itself to new possibilities, new instantiations, fresh determinations. Law in this dimension is incipiently pervasive and illimitable and is impelled into being by that which comes from beyond law's present positioning. Now, observations of contradictions or dualities in Foucault's thought are hardly uncommon in the critical literature. Indeed, as we saw in our Introduction, Foucault himself studiously cultivated an air of insouciant unconcern for consistency (in his famous riposte to the imagined 'bureaucrats' in *The Archaeology of Knowledge*, for example) which no doubt greatly added to the general impression of incoherence.[159] However, what we want to do now is to articulate these two opposed dimensions of Foucault's law not by way of correcting Foucault's inconsistency, but rather in the interests of observing a constitutive inconsistency – or *ir*resolution – in Foucault's theoretical object: law. In this light,

Foucault's astute theorization of the opposed dimensions of law appears wholly consistent.

Following the lead of the political theorist Jon Simons, who in *Foucault and the Political* explicitly locates Foucault's thought in that 'indeterminable, fluid space' between the 'two irreconcilable poles' of affirmative freedom and constraint,[160] we argue here that Foucault's law remains ever unresolved between the two dimensions of determinacy and responsiveness. What Foucault has identified in his various writings on law are two necessarily opposed yet co-implicated dimensions of the one *ir*resolute law. Put simply, law's determinacy is opposed to, yet requires, law's responsiveness, and vice versa. Whilst law in its determinate dimension must express a putatively definite content in order to secure the requisite order and predictability which it is called upon to guarantee, this legal determinacy must at the same time ever hold itself open to new domains of alterity and possibility. Law cannot simply 'be' a positivist creature of certitude, delimitation and calculation; rather, it must be capable of being something more than this, of being other to this determinacy, of being responsive. Even the maintenance of a determinate position or the calibration of a juridical rule necessitates a constant responsiveness to that which lies beyond the law's positioning or to that which the rule cannot presently comprise. Put crudely, law, if it is to rule effectively and secure the requisite certainty and predictability in the world beyond, must constantly relate to the ever-changing nature of society, the economy, and so forth. There is a constituent requirement for law to respond to the infinity of relation which can impinge upon its determinate position. And yet, whilst the law cannot simply ossify in the determinacy of its position, neither can it dissipate itself in a pure, unalloyed responsiveness to the other and to the changing world 'outside' it. This would equally be a failure of law since the law would dissolve in an impossible attempt to respond adequately to the singularity of the other and to incorporate diffuse forms and ways of being. There must perforce be determinate limits to law's responsiveness. We can see, then, that the determinacy of the law and the incipiently pervasive responsiveness of the law are not simply opposed but rather constitutively co-implicated, for the notion of a responsive law which incessantly disrupts itself in accommodating an other or an outside necessarily implies a determinate position from which the law can respond, whilst even the attempt to remain ostensibly the same requires at the very least a constant responsiveness to what lies beyond that position. Just as there can be no settled and determinate position without an ability to orient to a beyond, so can there be no orientation to a beyond without a determinate position from which to do so, and thence to return to. Moreover, if there were an enduring fixity of law there would be no more call for law, just as if there were a pure responsiveness the law would dissipate utterly. Foucault's law is unresolved between these two dimensions, and finds itself impelled by each in a contrary direction. More appositely, or at any rate in a more amenably Foucaultian idiom, we might say that the responsiveness of the law is *generative* or *productive* of law's determining, and vice versa. We perceive this bipartite 'unity' of Foucault's law in the incessant and unsettled movement from the one pole to the other, and back again, in law's 'im-possible, and yet necessary'[161] attempt to satisfy the imperatives of each.

In our reading of Foucault, then, law does not – to return to a question introduced towards the beginning of this section – simply aim to secure a determinate order. This is not, nor can it ever be, the sole 'work' of law.[162] Foucault's law, in its responsive dimension, must remain ever amenable to the ceaseless unmaking of any given order, to the very disordering of the present which, as we saw earlier, characterizes his mid-career reflections on the formative movement of power relations. As we have been arguing, there is a necessary, *constitutive* recalcitrance to Foucault's law. Accordingly, in a number of texts Foucault makes an explicit distinction between law and order. Our first example comes from the end of the lecture, 'The Political Technology of Individuals', in which Foucault argues for the impossibility of reducing law to the imperatives of order. Indeed, in this lecture he even asserts that there exists an 'antinomy' between the two concepts.[163] Something of law is lost, Foucault seems to argue, in law's complete subordination to the exigencies of order:

> Law, by definition, is always referred to a juridical system, and order is referred to an administrative system, to a state's specific order, which was exactly the idea of all those utopians of the beginning of the seventeenth century and was also the idea of those very real administrators of the eighteenth century. I think that the conciliation between law and order, which has been the dream of those men, must remain a dream. It's impossible to reconcile law and order because when you try to do so it is only in the form of an integration of law into the state's order.[164]

Foucault repeats the theme in a review of journalist Philippe Boucher's book, *Le Ghetto judiciare*, where he explicitly holds open a conceptual space between law, on the one hand, and the production and maintenance of social order, on the other. Writing of the founding in 1968 of the progressive French magistrate's trade union, the Syndicat de la magistrature, Foucault observes:

> It has often been said that the Syndicat de la magistrature wanted to 'politicize' the administration of justice. I would be inclined to think rather the opposite: it wanted to bring the question of law to bear on a certain 'policy' of justice which was that of order. 'Law and Order' is not simply the motto of American conservatism, it is a hybridized monster. Those who fight for human rights are well aware of this. As for those who have forgotten that fact, Philippe Boucher's book will remind them of it. Just as people say milk or lemon, we should say law *or* order. It is up to us to draw lessons for the future from that incompatibility.[165]

What might be lost, Foucault suggests in the above discussions of law's integration into order, is the law's suscitating ability to be otherwise than it is, to responsively (and self-disruptively) open itself to the singularity of the other and the infinite, unstilled possibilities of the outside. And yet − Foucault also recognizes − it is ultimately 'impossible'[166] to effect such reconciliation, for law in its self-resistant, responsive dimension is inimical to such containment. This responsiveness is the shifting margin by which Foucault's law must necessarily exceed itself if it is to remain law; it is that necessary process whereby 'the law is inverted and passes outside itself'.[167] Foucault's law, like his more famous descriptions of power relations in modernity, thus reveals its constitutive reliance upon an 'instability' which opposes any concrete order.[168]

However, with law's constituently holding itself open to new ways of being it necessarily reveals its very lack of determinate and enduring content. Law's illimitable responsiveness means that it cannot assume any set content and hence it is ultimately a vacuity. It is this constituently vacuous aspect of law with which we want to close our discussion in this chapter, relating it to some of the criticisms mounted by adherents of the 'expulsion thesis' to the effect that Foucault instrumentally subordinates law to power. As we shall see, Foucault's law is indeed made the instrument of powers external and seemingly superordinate to it, and to this extent we can concede some limited purchase to these critical readings. However, what we hope to show in the concluding discussion to this chapter is that the dimension of Foucault's law which most facilitates its instrumental subordination by power − its responsiveness − in fact also renders impossible a total(itarian) comprehension by power. In short, as we have been observing, Foucault's law eludes containment.

LAW'S POLYVALENT VACUITY

If there is a 'violence done to the law',[169]and if law is inescapably '"subject to [the] orders"' of a predominant power,[170] then this instrumentalization of law flows necessarily from its responsive dimension. The constituent force of law's responsiveness, its illimitable opening of itself to new possibilities and new forms, leaves the law with a vacuity of enduring content. For law incipiently to be other to its present instantiation, it cannot be definitively tied to any singular and determinate form. '[L]aw itself', observes Jean-Luc Nancy, 'does not have a form for what would need to be its own sovereignty.'[171] Lacking a form of its own, having in fact a 'total lack of content',[172] law also lacks a history. Indeed, as Derrida observes, it 'seems to exclude all historicity':[173]

> It seems that the law as such should never give rise to any story. To be invested with its categorical authority, the law must be without history, genesis, or any possible derivation. That would be *the law of the law*.[174]

In this sense, Bob Fine is correct in arguing that Foucault reduces the law to an 'empty form'.[175] Indeed, Foucault consistently observes law's vacuity. From the 'gaps' and 'silences' of the law to its 'empty' areas,[176] law frequently appears (or, perhaps, dis-appears) in his writings as an 'impalpable substance',[177] as a present 'absence'.[178] Indeed, as he writes in the essay 'Nietzsche, Genealogy, History', 'rules are empty in themselves'. This of course has the consequence for law that, as the quotation continues, 'they are made to serve this or that, and can be bent to any purpose'.[179] It is in its constituent emptiness, then, in its very lack of perduring and determinate content, that law is inherently amenable to appropriation and instrumentalization by external powers. Foucault provides ample evidence of such instrumentalization, also. In past lives the law was once 'skillfully wielded by monarchs',[180] and indeed prior to the age of governmentality the laws were the predominant 'instruments of government'.[181] In modernity law's subjection continues – law is still reduced to playing the role of accessory, instrument or support of the new bio-powers, to providing cover for them or making them 'acceptable'.[182] Law's instrumental subordination is seemingly confirmed in its needing always to be enforced by something or somebody apart from it. Thus, Foucault writes in *Discipline and Punish* that 'the force of the law is the force of the prince'.[183] Indeed, the majesty and splendour of the public spectacles of the pre-modern period demonstrated, in somewhat bloodthirsty fashion, that the law derived its force precisely

from the monarch who exercised it: '[t]he ceremony of the public torture and execution displayed for all to see the power relation that gave
his force to the law'.[184] These sanguinary ceremonies of 'armed justice'[185]
illustrate not an excessive law but rather a supine law, a law which is
necessarily dependent on powers apart from itself to give it some effect.
As Foucault says, the law 'functions and justifies itself only by this perpetual reference to something other than itself'.[186] If, when we encounter
it in its pre-modern instantiations, '[l]aw cannot help but but [sic] be
armed',[187] this is not so much because it is necessarily physically violent
but rather because it needs to be executed from elsewhere; it must needs
'refer to the sword' in order to operate.[188] And Foucault shows us, with
admirable continuity, how law in modernity cannot be self-executing
either; indeed, how it cannot be 'the master of its truth'.[189] Law has been
penetrated by the normalizing powers of discipline, whose 'assessing,
diagnostic, prognostic, normative judgments concerning the criminal
have become lodged in the framework of penal judgment'.[190] These new
powers come, as we have seen, to 'gradually ... invade the major [legal]
forms, altering their mechanisms and imposing their procedures'.[191] Again,
'the techniques of discipline and discourses born of discipline are invading
right, and ... normalizing procedures are increasingly colonizing the
procedures of the law'.[192] If the law in all this seems strangely 'hospitable'[193] to the intervention and control of the new power formations,
to the 'emergence of the not-legal ... within legality itself',[194] it is because
these interventions are not anomalous or dangerous but are in fact
'operational mechanisms'.[195] Simply, this is how law works – it is
always subject to and applied by power. 'The law', as Foucault tells us, 'is
applied by and through ... the requirements of a [political] interest.'[196]
Law is thoroughly dependent upon powers beyond it, whether those
powers represent the prerogatives of monarchical sovereignty or the
imperatives of a disciplinary or bio-political formation, to give it content
and purchase. In regard to these superordinate powers the law is 'fragile,
permeable, and transparent. ... It is "as flexible as one pleases".'[197]

And yet this vacuous flexibility would simply go to confirm the subordinated law for which Foucault is criticized in the 'expulsion thesis',
were it not for the fact that in its vacuity the responsive law cannot
ultimately be contained by any given power. The vacuity of Foucault's
law is a polyvalent vacuity, an insubordinate openness, for the 'strategic
reversibility'[198] of Foucault's law consists precisely in the fact that what
makes it open to appropriation and domination simultaneously makes it
open to a resignification and renewal that eludes the determination of a
sovereign or a given regime of power. It is in this light that we can
understand Foucault's insistence in *Discipline and Punish* that whilst the

disciplines, to return to a quotation we discussed in the first section of this chapter, 'effect a suspension of the law' that is 'never annulled', nevertheless they do not manage to make such a suspension 'total'.[199] Foucault's law is both presently containable and yet ultimately uncontainable; its rules are applied in the interests of an occupying power yet, crucially, these same rules remain ever 'unfinalized'.[200]

CONCLUSION

In this chapter we have attempted to engage with the 'expulsion thesis' which we explored in Chapter 1. We first demonstrated that, contrary to reports of its expulsion or demise, law in fact remains a persistent feature of Foucault's portrayals of modernity. Indeed, in discussing the relationship which Foucault describes between law and disciplinary power, we sought to show how in fact disciplinary power, far from suppressing or expelling law, was actually thoroughly dependent upon it. More importantly, however, we sought in the second part of the chapter to derive from Foucault a much more complex, poststructuralist conception of law itself. We showed how Foucault isolates two opposed dimensions of law, and that it is in the unsettled articulation of these two opposed yet co-implicated dimensions that modern law finds its labile 'place'. This law is susceptible to instrumentalization by seemingly preponderant powers and yet at the same time holds itself ever open to unthought possibilities. In being 'neither the truth of power nor its alibi',[201] Foucault's law must retain the possibility of being ever other than what it is. In the next chapter, we develop and extend our theme of the combination of a present determinacy and a responsiveness to what lies beyond, and we argue for a more central and constituent placing of law in Foucault's modernity. Through the idea of the 'law of the law', we argue that Foucault's law – in its iterative ability to combine a present determinacy with an incorporative orientation to a beyond – constitutes the very social bond of modernity, the means of our relation and being-with each other.

Thus far we have moved from our discussion in Chapter 1 of the orthodox reception of Foucault on law (namely, his having relegated law to a position of inferiority or irrelevance) to articulating in the present chapter our own understanding of Foucault's law. What we now want to achieve in our final chapter, 'completing' this trajectory, is a more robust reversal of the orthodoxy that Foucault marginalized and downplayed law's importance. To the contrary, we want to place Foucault's law at the constituent core of the social bond. In so doing, we shall relate Foucault's thinking on law to some of his other, perhaps better known, reflections upon ethics and critical ontology. Throughout our discussion, however, our emphasis and orientation shall remain on law, on a law that, in its insistent capacity to be otherwise than what it is, provides society with a 'means for a future or a truth that it will not know and that it will not be'.[202]

Notes

1 Michel Foucault, 'The End of the Monarchy of Sex', in *Foucault Live: Collected Interviews, 1961–1984*, trans. Lysa Hochroth and John Johnston, ed. Sylvère Lotringer (New York: Semiotext(e), 1989), pp. 214–25 (p. 225).

2 Michel Foucault, 'Maurice Blanchot: The Thought from Outside', trans. Brian Massumi, in *Foucault/Blanchot* (New York: Zone Books, 1987), pp. 9–58; Michel Foucault, 'A Preface to Transgression', in *Language, Counter-Memory, Practice: Selected Essays and Interviews*, trans. Donald F. Bouchard and Sherry Simon, ed. Donald F. Bouchard (Ithaca, NY: Cornell University Press, 1977), pp. 29–52.

3 Paul Q. Hirst, *Law, Socialism and Democracy* (London: Allen & Unwin, 1986), p. 49.

4 Michel Foucault, *The Archaeology of Knowledge*, trans. A. M. Sheridan Smith (London: Routledge, 1972), p. 4.

5 Michel Foucault, *The Will to Knowledge: The History of Sexuality, Vol. 1*, trans. Robert Hurley (Harmondsworth: Penguin, 1979), p. 144.

6 *Ibid.*, p. 144.

7 Ann Laura Stoler, *Race and the Education of Desire: Foucault's* History of Sexuality *and the Colonial Order of Things* (Durham, NC: Duke University Press, 1995), p. 38.

8 Foucault, *The History of Sexuality, Vol. 1*, p. 147.

9 *Ibid.*, p. 148 (emphasis in original). Foucault frequently employs the historical periodization of the Renaissance, the classical age and modernity in his work, although the precision with which the start of the respective time periods is rendered varies slightly from work to work. For example, the division between the Renaissance, the classical era, and modernity is relied upon in his *History of Madness*. In this text, Foucault is quite precise about the timing of the respective periods. The experience of madness in the Renaissance ends with the birth of the classical era, which Foucault dates to the founding of the Hôpital Général in 1657, whilst the modern experience of madness is dated to Pinel's liberation of the mad from Bicêtre in 1794. See Michel Foucault, *History of Madness*, trans. Jonathan Murphy and Jean Khalfa (Abingdon: Routledge, 2006), p. xxxiii. In *The Order of Things*, by contrast, Foucault dates the commencement of the classical age to 'roughly half-way through the seventeenth century' and the commencement of the modern era from 'the beginning of the nineteenth century'. See Michel Foucault, *The Order of Things: An Archaeology of the Human Sciences*, trans. Alan Sheridan (New York: Vintage Books, 1994), p. xxii.

10 Foucault, *The History of Sexuality, Vol. 1*, p. 149. For another example of this tendency, compare *The History of Sexuality, Vol. 1*, in which Foucault

states that the old sovereign right to take life is 'replaced' by the new bio-political right to foster life (p. 138), but where the context of his discussion clearly indicates that both modalities of power co-exist. See also Michel Foucault, *'Society Must Be Defended': Lectures at the Collège de France, 1975–76*, trans. David Macey (London: Allen Lane, 2003), p. 241, where he argues that the old sovereign right is not in fact replaced but rather 'complemented' and that the new right comes to 'penetrate it' and 'permeate it' rather than supersede it.

11 Michel Foucault, *Security, Territory, Population: Lectures at the Collège de France 1977–78*, trans. Graham Burchell (Basingstoke: Palgrave Macmillan, 2007), p. 107. See Chapter 1, note 103 for a history of the separate translation and publication of the 'Governmentality' lecture. In the first lecture of the series, dated 11 January 1978, Foucault gives a clearer account of how juridical or legal techniques, disciplinary techniques, and apparatuses of security co-exist and are overlaid (see pp. 6–8).

12 Foucault is of course read by many people as a, perhaps *the*, historian of discontinuity. His early archaeological approach to history (as practised, for example, in a text like *The Order of Things*) has been criticized for focusing solely upon epistemological breaks and discontinuities and for not offering a plausible theory of historical change. The most famous critique of *The Order of Things* along these lines was that of Jean-Paul Sartre, who argued that Foucault had, in substituting the random discontinuity of structures for the dialectical movement of history, 'replace[d] the motion picture with the magic lantern, movement with a succession of immobilities' (Jean-Paul Sartre, 'Jean-Paul Sartre répond', *L'Arc*, 30 October 1966, p. 87, quoted and translated in Eric Paras, *Foucault 2.0: Beyond Power and Knowledge* (New York: Other Press, 2006), p. 30). For Foucault's response to readings of *The Order of Things* which stress its discontinuity, see Michel Foucault, 'On Power', in *Politics, Philosophy, Culture: Interviews and Other Writings, 1977–1984*, trans. Alan Sheridan *et al.*, ed. Lawrence D. Kritzman (London: Routledge, 1988), pp. 96–109 (pp. 99–100). In this interview Foucault stresses that his project in *The Order of Things* was to explain the epistemic transformations necessary in order for discursive ruptures to take place; that is, precisely an attempt to 'resolve' the 'problem' of discontinuity (p. 100). On this question, see also Michel Foucault, 'Politics and the Study of Discourse', trans. Colin Gordon, in *The Foucault Effect: Studies in Governmentality*, ed. Graham Burchell, Colin Gordon and Peter Miller (Chicago: University of Chicago Press, 1991), pp. 53–72 (pp. 58–59); Michel Foucault, 'Truth and Power', in *Power/Knowledge: Selected Interviews and Other Writings 1972–1977*, trans. Colin Gordon *et al.*, ed. Colin Gordon (Brighton: Harvester Press, 1980), pp. 109–33 (pp. 111–13). For an interesting and sensitive discussion of Foucault's historical method which likewise dispels 'certain preconceived notions about the philosopher', chief among them the belief that '[Foucault] privileges breaks and structures over continuities and evolutions', see Paul Veyne, 'Foucault Revolutionizes History', trans. Catherine Porter, in *Foucault and his Interlocutors*, ed. Arnold I. Davidson (Chicago and London: University of Chicago Press, 1997), pp. 146–82 (p. 146). Finally, for a succinct discussion of Foucault's later genealogical method and its Nietzschean antecedents, see Michel Foucault, 'Nietzsche, Genealogy, History', in *Essential Works of Foucault 1954–1984*,

Vol. 2: Aesthetics, Method, and Epistemology, trans. Robert Hurley *et al.*,
ed. James Faubion (Harmondsworth: Penguin, 2000), pp. 369–91.

13 George Pavlich, *Governing Paradoxes of Restorative Justice* (London:
GlassHouse Press, 2005), p. 9.

14 See Foucault, *The History of Sexuality, Vol. 1*, p. 144. As Foucault's comments
on the state, and his later work on governmentality and on forms of political
rationality, make clear, he never excluded the state from his analysis. Rather,
the state remains very much a significant site for the generation and orga-
nizing of power (even if it is not always foregrounded in this way). See our
discussion in the section 'The governmentality of law' in Chapter 1, especially our discussion of this point in note 121.

15 *Ibid.*, p. 90.

16 For example, see Gary Wickham, 'Foucault and Law', in *An Introduction
to Law and Social Theory*, ed. Reza Banakar and Max Travers (Oxford:
Hart, 2002), pp. 249–65 (p. 250). In this discussion Wickham analyses a similar
quotation from Foucault, *The History of Sexuality, Vol. 1*, p. 102.

17 Foucault, *The History of Sexuality, Vol. 1*, p. 90.

18 *Ibid.*, p. 89. See also Foucault, 'Truth and Power', p. 121.

19 Foucault, *The History of Sexuality, Vol. 1*, p. 97.

20 Foucault, *Security, Territory, Population*, p. 106.

21 *Ibid.*, p. 107. As Brian Singer and Lorna Weir rightly observe, 'Foucault
nowhere maintained that governmentality abolished sovereignty' (Brian C.
J. Singer and Lorna Weir, 'Politics and Sovereign Power: Considerations on
Foucault' (2006) 9 *European Journal of Social Theory* 443, 448).

22 Michel Foucault, 'What is Called "Punishing"?', in *Essential Works of
Foucault 1954–1984, Vol. 3: Power*, trans. Robert Hurley *et al.*, ed. James
D. Faubion (New York: New Press, 2000), pp. 382–93 (p. 392).

23 Michel Foucault, *Discipline and Punish: The Birth of the Prison*, trans. Alan
Sheridan (Harmondsworth: Penguin, 1991), p. 223.

24 Nikolas Rose and Mariana Valverde, 'Governed by Law?' (1998) 7 *Social &
Legal Studies* 541, 542. Here 'norm' is being used in the specifically extra-
legal sense which Foucault developed in his writings on disciplinary power
in the mid-1970s. See our discussion in Chapter 1, note 43.

25 Anthony Beck, 'Foucault and Law: The Collapse of Law's Empire' (1996)
16 *Oxford Journal of Legal Studies* 489, 494.

26 Foucault, '*Society Must Be Defended*', pp. 37–38.

27 Foucault, *Discipline and Punish*, p. 216. In this passage Foucault does not
expressly mention law. The passage begins thus: 'Not because the disciplinary
modality of power has replaced all the others; but because it has infiltrated
the others, sometimes undermining them, but serving as an intermediary
between them … '. Nevertheless, we argue for two reasons that Foucault
intends to include law within the phrase 'other' powers here. First, elsewhere
in *Discipline and Punish* the phrase 'other powers', used by Foucault to designate modalities of power other than the disciplinary, explicitly encompasses law
(for example, see *Discipline and Punish*, p. 184). Second, the way in which
Foucault figures the relation between the 'other' powers and discipline
(whereby the latter 'sometimes undermin[es]' the former), recalls Foucault's
more explicit formulations of the relation between law and discipline – for
example, see *ibid.*, p. 170; Foucault, *Security, Territory, Population*, p. 56.

28 Foucault, *History of Madness*, p. xxviii.

29 Foucault, *Discipline and Punish*, p. 19.
30 *Ibid.*, p. 23.
31 *Ibid.*, p. 28.
32 *Ibid.*, p. 23. On the question of matrices, see Panu Minkkinen, 'The Juridical Matrix' (1997) 6 *Social & Legal Studies* 425.
33 Foucault, *Discipline and Punish*, p. 183.
34 For a classic instance, see Hans Kelsen, *Pure Theory of Law*, 2nd edn, trans. Max Knight (Berkeley and Los Angeles: University of California Press, 1967), p. 1 ('It is called a "pure" theory of law, because it only describes the law and attempts to eliminate from the object of this description everything that is not strictly law: Its aim is to free the science of law from alien elements. This is the methodological basis of the theory').
35 Foucault, *Discipline and Punish*, p. 222.
36 *Ibid.*, p. 227.
37 *Ibid.*, p. 305.
38 *Ibid.*, p. 191.
39 *Ibid.*, p. 193.
40 It is important to recall that Foucault, in his work on power and knowledge (or, 'power-knowledge'), posited an intricate and symbiotic link between the two notions – and *not* an identity between them: 'It has been said but you have to understand that when I read – and I know it has been attributed to me – the thesis, "Knowledge is power," or "Power is knowledge," I begin to laugh, since studying their *relation* is precisely my problem. If they were identical, I would not have to study them and I would be spared a lot of fatigue as a result. The very fact that I pose the question of their relation proves clearly that I do not *identify* them.' See Michel Foucault, 'Critical Theory/ Intellectual History', in *Politics, Philosophy, Culture*, pp. 17–46 (p. 43) (emphasis in original).
41 Foucault, *Discipline and Punish*, p. 193.
42 *Ibid.*, p. 193.
43 Foucault, *'Society Must Be Defended'*, p. 25.
44 Much of Foucault's work, especially his mid-1970s work on power, is a critique of the human sciences and the mobilization of scientific status and notions of truth within the discourses of the human sciences.
45 Foucault, *Discipline and Punish*, p. 296.
46 *Ibid.*, p. 302.
47 See Jan Goldstein, 'Framing Discipline with Law: Problems and Promises of the Liberal State' (1993) 98 *American Historical Review* 364.
48 Various legal developments subsequent to the case we consider here, developments such as the passing of criminal justice legislation and the enactment of the *Human Rights Act 1998* (UK) (as well as domestic and European case law interpreting this Act), have modified both the position of prisoners and the nature of these disciplinary hearings. For example, the *Criminal Justice Act 1991* (UK) removed the role of the Board of Visitors in hearing disciplinary charges, whilst one of the results of the coming into effect of the *Human Rights Act 1998* (UK) in 2000 has been that prison inmates can make domestic challenges to the manner of their disciplinary hearings based on the right to a fair trial (Article 6 of the *European Convention on Human Rights* as given expression municipally by the *Human Rights Act 1998* (UK)). For a recent judicial discussion of the extent to which the right to a fair trial is

engaged, and what it imports in the context of disciplinary hearings, see the judgment of the Court of Appeal for England and Wales in *Tangney v The Governor of HMP Elmley and Anor*. [2005] EWCA Civ 1009.

49 1988 AC 379 (hereinafter *Hone*).
50 *Becker v Home Office and Another* 1972 2 QB 407, at 418.
51 *Hone*, at 392.
52 *Ibid.*, at 392.
53 *Ibid.*, at 392.
54 *Ibid.*, at 392. For a related, Foucaultian analysis of the judicial review of administrative action, see Anne Barron, 'Legal Discourse and the Colonisation of the Self in the Modern State', in *Post-Modern Law: Enlightenment, Revolution and the Death of Man*, ed. Anthony Carty (Edinburgh: Edinburgh University Press, 1990), pp. 107–25 (pp. 118–19).
55 Foucault, *Discipline and Punish*, p. 193.
56 *Ibid.*, p. 256.
57 *Ibid.*, p. 106.
58 *Ibid.*, p. 66.
59 *Ibid.*, pp. 296, 302.
60 Foucault, *'Society Must Be Defended'*, p. 37.
61 In doing this it not only allows disciplinary power to 'fabricate' the disciplined and docile subject (Foucault, *Discipline and Punish*, p. 308), but also benefits greatly in return from this disciplinary production of the self-responsible individual, an individual who would internalize norms of submission and deference to (legal) authority. Unable in its modern, self-limiting liberal rendition to reach into the 'extremities', the 'outer limits', the 'capillary' points of disciplinary power's operation in society (*ibid.*, p. 27), law receives a subject pre-adapted for legality by disciplinary power (on this topic, see also Foucault's discussion of the legal fiction of the workshop contract, *ibid.*, p. 223).
62 *Ibid.*, p. 223.
63 *Ibid.*, p. 296.
64 *Ibid.*, pp. 202–03.
65 Michel Foucault, 'What is Critique?', trans. Kevin Paul Geiman, in *What is Enlightenment? Eighteenth-Century Answers and Twentieth-Century Questions*, ed. James Schmidt (Berkeley and Los Angeles: University of California Press, 1996), pp. 382–98 (p. 386).
66 Michel Foucault, 'Powers and Strategies', in *Power/Knowledge*, pp. 134–45 (p. 138).
67 Foucault, *The History of Sexuality, Vol. 1*, p. 143.
68 Michel Foucault, '"Omnes et Singulatim": Toward a Critique of Political Reason', in *Essential Works of Foucault, Vol. 3: Power*, pp. 298–325 (p. 312).
69 Foucault, 'What is Critique?', p. 386. As Pavlich explains, 'critical opposition to governance enters a politics of truth precisely when it contests problematic subject identities (singular or collective) that are basic to given governmentalities'. See George Pavlich, *Critique and Radical Discourses on Crime* (Aldershot: Ashgate, 2000), pp. 103–04.
70 Foucault, 'Powers and Strategies', p. 138.
71 Foucault, *Discipline and Punish*, p. 268.
72 Michel Foucault, 'The Subject and Power', in *Essential Works of Foucault, Vol. 3: Power*, pp. 326–48 (p. 342).

73 Foucault, 'Powers and Strategies', p. 138.
74 On the distinction between law and norm, see Chapter 1, note 43. On the historical contingency of the distinction between state administration (as a site of disciplinary power) and law, see Harry Arthurs, 'Without the Law': Administrative Justice and Legal Pluralism in Nineteenth-Century England (Toronto: University of Toronto Press, 1985).
75 Foucault, Discipline and Punish, pp. 177–78.
76 Ibid., p. 178.
77 Ibid., p. 222.
78 Ibid., p. 304.
79 Foucault, 'Society Must Be Defended', p. 38.
80 Foucault, Discipline and Punish, p. 303.
81 Ibid., pp. 221–22.
82 Ibid., p. 255.
83 Michel Foucault, 'Lemon and Milk', in Essential Works of Foucault, Vol. 3: Power, pp. 435–38 (p. 437).
84 Foucault, Discipline and Punish, p. 17.
85 Foucault, The History of Sexuality, Vol. 1, p. 93.
86 Ibid., p. 92.
87 Foucault, 'Truth and Power', p. 119.
88 Foucault, 'Powers and Strategies', p. 139.
89 Foucault, The History of Sexuality, Vol. 1, p. 84.
90 Michel Foucault, The Use of Pleasure: The History of Sexuality, Vol. 2, trans. Robert Hurley (Harmondsworth: Penguin, 1992), p. 250.
91 Foucault, Security, Territory, Population, p. 47.
92 Of course, the trope of law as measurement is hardly an original Foucaultian notion. See Foucault's early interest in studying classical Greek notions of the 'nomos, a just law of distribution ensuring the order of the city-state by making an order reign therein which is the order of the world' (Michel Foucault, 'The Will to Knowledge', in Essential Works of Foucault 1954–1984, Vol. 1: Ethics, Subjectivity and Truth, trans. Robert Hurley et al., ed. Paul Rabinow (Harmondsworth: Allen Lane/Penguin, 1997), pp. 11–16 (p. 15) (emphasis in original)). On the trope of law as measurement in Foucault, see Steven Mailloux, 'Measuring Justice: Notes on Fish, Foucault, and the Law' (1997) 9 Cardozo Studies in Law and Literature 1; John Frow, 'Measure for Measure: A Response to Steven Mailloux' (1997) 9 Cardozo Studies in Law and Literature 11.
93 Foucault, 'Lemon and Milk', p. 437.
94 Foucault, Security, Territory, Population, p. 46.
95 Of course, on occasions Foucault disclaimed any intention to theorize about power. For example, in the interview 'Critical Theory/Intellectual History', Foucault comments: 'I am far from being a theoretician of power. At the limit, I would say that power, as an autonomous question, does not interest me. ... I am not developing a theory of power' (Foucault, 'Critical Theory/ Intellectual History', p. 39). Whilst he may not have been attempting to formulate a general or universal theory of power abstracted from its various social instantiations, nevertheless, as the above discussion in the text illustrates, he does theorize power at some length in certain key works in the 1970s and early 1980s. In so doing, his emphasis is on the manner in which power is exercised in a diverse range of institutional and social locations

(disciplinary power, bio-power, governmentality, and so forth). That is, Foucault was dedicated to '[s]tudying the "how" of power ... [by] trying to understand its mechanisms' (Foucault, *'Society Must Be Defended'*, p. 24). On the question of Foucault's approach to theory, see the discussion in our Introduction (in the text accompanying notes 8–23).

96 Foucault, *The History of Sexuality, Vol. 1*, p. 93.
97 *Ibid.*, p. 93.
98 *Ibid.*, p. 93.
99 *Ibid.*, p. 93.
100 *Ibid.*, p. 82.
101 See Foucault, *'Society Must Be Defended'*, pp. 13–14.
102 Foucault, *The History of Sexuality, Vol. 1*, p. 94.
103 Foucault, *'Society Must Be Defended'*, p. 29.
104 Foucault, *The History of Sexuality, Vol. 1*, p. 94.
105 See our discussion of Marxist and feminist criticisms of Foucault on this score in Chapter 1, note 121. For a particularly obtuse rendition of this criticism, see Michael Walzer, 'The Politics of Michel Foucault', in *Foucault: A Critical Reader*, ed. David Couzens Hoy (Oxford: Blackwell, 1986), pp. 51–68 (p. 66).
106 Foucault, *The History of Sexuality, Vol. 1*, p. 93.
107 *Ibid.*, p. 93.
108 Foucault, *Discipline and Punish*, p. 301.
109 Michel Foucault, 'Sex, Power, and the Politics of Identity', in *Essential Works of Foucault, Vol. 1: Ethics*, pp. 163–73 (p. 167). The phrase was popularized by Gilles Deleuze, *Foucault*, trans. Seán Hand (London: Continuum, 1999), p. 74: 'Moreover, the final word on power is that *resistance comes first*' (emphasis in original). On the 'primacy of resistance', see also Michael Hardt and Antonio Negri, *Multitude: War and Democracy in the Age of Empire* (London: Hamish Hamilton, 2004), p. 64.
110 Foucault, *The History of Sexuality, Vol. 1*, p. 95.
111 *Ibid.*, p. 93.
112 *Ibid.*, p. 95.
113 *Ibid.*, p. 96.
114 *Ibid.*, p. 95.
115 *Ibid.*, p. 95.
116 Foucault, 'Powers and Strategies', p. 138.
117 Foucault, *The History of Sexuality, Vol. 1*, p. 96.
118 *Ibid.*, p. 95.
119 *Ibid.*, p. 101.
120 *Ibid.*, p. 95.
121 Foucault, 'The Subject and Power', p. 342.
122 See George Pavlich, 'The Art of Critique or How Not to be Governed Thus', in *Rethinking Law, Society and Governance: Foucault's Bequest*, ed. Gary Wickham and George Pavlich (Oxford: Hart, 2001), pp. 141–54 (p. 147).
123 Foucault, 'The Subject and Power', p. 329.
124 *Ibid.*, p. 329.
125 The oft-quoted example is Clifford Geertz's observation of *Discipline and Punish* that it described 'a kind of Whig history in reverse – a history, in spite of itself, of the Rise of Unfreedom', quoted in David Couzens Hoy, 'Introduction', in *Foucault: A Critical Reader*, pp. 1–25 (p. 11). Suffice it to

say that such teleologies, either of despair or of inexorable progress, are utterly foreign to Foucault's genealogical approach to writing history. For an excellent discussion of the nuances and radical nature of Foucault's approach, see Véronique Voruz, 'The Politics of *The Culture of Control*: Undoing Genealogy' (2005) 34 *Economy and Society* 154.

126 Foucault, 'The Subject and Power', p. 343.

127 Foucault, 'Powers and Strategies', p. 138.

128 *Ibid.*, p. 138.

129 Foucault, *The History of Sexuality, Vol. 1*, p. 97.

130 Foucault, 'Sex, Power, and the Politics of Identity', p. 167.

131 As for not equating transgression with the later formulation of resistance, a further caveat may perhaps be useful here, which is that Foucault's championing of the language of transgression is significantly modified in some of his later writings. Whereas Foucault argued in 'A Preface to Transgression', p. 33, that 'the language in which transgression will find its space and the illumination of its being almost entirely in the future' and that in Bataille one can perceive 'its calcinated roots, its promising ashes', with the publication of the first volume of *The History of Sexuality* Foucault comes to view the language of transgression as outdated. He argues that 'conceiv[ing] the category of the sexual in terms of the law, death, blood, and sovereignty ... is in the last analysis a historical "retro-version". We must conceptualize the deployment of sexuality on the basis of the techniques of power that are contemporary with it' (*The History of Sexuality, Vol. 1*, p. 150). Two pages earlier in the same text, Foucault makes clear that transgression is allied with the outmoded concepts of law, death, blood, and sovereignty: 'The new procedures of power that were devised during the classical age and employed in the nineteenth century were what caused our societies to go from *a symbolics of blood* to *an analytics of sexuality*. Clearly, nothing was more on the side of the law, death, transgression, the symbolic, and sovereignty than blood; just as sexuality was on the side of the norm, knowledge, life, meaning, the disciplines, and regulations' (p. 148; emphasis in original). However, whilst Foucault seems to distance himself from his earlier positions on transgression, he continues to thematize the notions of exteriority and the necessity of an engagement with alterity well into his late work, and it is this impetus and theoretical dynamic that will prove important for our argument here.

132 Foucault, 'A Preface to Transgression', p. 32.

133 *Ibid.*, p. 34.

134 *Ibid.*, p. 34.

135 *Ibid.*, p. 35.

136 *Ibid.*, p. 35.

137 *Ibid.*, p. 34.

138 *Ibid.*, p. 35.

139 *Ibid.*, p. 34.

140 *Ibid.*, p. 34.

141 *Ibid.*, p. 34.

142 *Ibid.*, p. 34.

143 *Ibid.*, p. 32.

144 From our discussions so far and in the text below, we hope it will be evident that our usage of 'responsiveness' in regard to law differs in several important

respects from the deployment of that term, also in regard to law, by Philippe Nonet and Philip Selznick, *Law and Society in Transition: Toward Responsive Law* (New Brunswick, NJ: Transaction Publishers, 2001). In their neo-Weberian analysis of law in its historical development, law progresses from a *repressive* stage, to an *autonomous* stage, and then finally to a *responsive* stage. For Nonet and Selznick, then, these attributes of law define its mode of being at a given stage in its development, and are not, and as we would argue to the contrary, co-implicated simultaneous dimensions of the one law. Moreover, for Nonet and Selznick, the 'responsiveness' of law equates, in the end result, to a philosophically pragmatic position. This position reduces law to an instrument of public policy, whereas with our usage 'responsiveness' is intended to convey *both* law's instrumental reduction *and yet* its inability to be ultimately captured in this way.

145 Foucault, 'Maurice Blanchot: The Thought from Outside', p. 38.
146 *Ibid.*, p. 34.
147 *Ibid.*, p. 36.
148 *Ibid.*, p. 38.
149 *Ibid.*, p. 34.
150 Maurice Blanchot, *The Step Not Beyond*, trans. Lycette Nelson (Albany, NY: State University of New York Press, 1992), p. 24.
151 Maurice Blanchot, *The Infinite Conversation*, trans. Susan Hanson (Minneapolis and London: University of Minnesota Press, 1993), p. 434. We note at this point that some Foucault scholars expressly disregard Foucault's early work on literature and on modernist aesthetics in which he engages with, among others, Maurice Blanchot and Georges Bataille – engagements which are key to our reading of Foucault in this book. For example, John Rajchman, *Michel Foucault: The Freedom of Philosophy* (New York: Columbia University Press, 1985), p. 29, argues that Foucault's engagements with literature in the 1960s are of little use in coming to terms with his more mature work on power and ethics because in the later work Foucault jettisons his earlier aesthetic concerns and interests in favour of more practical political engagements. For us, however, whilst Foucault departs from the use of certain themes and tropes (for example, see note 131, above, on transgression) the engagement with exteriority (an engagement we have focused upon here in terms of law and its relationship to its outside) continues into his later work and is central to it. Moreover, in our perceiving a thematic continuity between the early material on literature and aesthetics and the later work on power and ethics, we have specifically integrated our discussion of the earlier work with our treatment of his central texts of the mid-1970s and early 1980s. Finally, for a Derridean-inspired argument that the concept of exteriority (as pursued in the engagement with Blanchot herein discussed) is central to an understanding of Foucault's late work on ethics, indeed that it 'haunts' it, see Kas Saghafi, 'The "Passion for the Outside": Foucault, Blanchot, and Exteriority' (1996) 28 *International Studies in Philosophy* 79.
152 Jerry D. Leonard, 'Foucault: Genealogy, Law, Praxis' (1990) 14 *Legal Studies Forum* 3, 11. See also Jerry Leonard, 'Foucault and (the Ideology of) Genealogical Legal Theory', in *Legal Studies as Cultural Studies: A Reader in (Post)Modern Critical Theory*, ed. Jerry D. Leonard (Albany, NY: State University of New York Press, 1995), pp. 133–51 (pp. 140–41).
153 Foucault, *The History of Sexuality, Vol. 1*, p. 97.

154 Foucault, 'Maurice Blanchot: The Thought from Outside', p. 34.
155 Foucault, *Discipline and Punish*, p. 22.
156 Foucault, 'Maurice Blanchot: The Thought from Outside', p. 34.
157 See Foucault, *Discipline and Punish*, p. 170; Foucault, *'Society Must Be Defended'*, p. 38.
158 Jon Simons, *Foucault and the Political* (London: Routledge, 1995), p. 83.
159 Foucault, *The Archaeology of Knowledge*, p. 17.
160 Simons, *Foucault and the Political*, pp. 5, 3.
161 Jacques Derrida, *Rogues: Two Essays on Reason*, trans. Pascale-Anne Brault and Michael Naas (Stanford, CA: Stanford University Press, 2005), p. 84. Readers familiar with the writings of Jacques Derrida on law will no doubt perceive resonances between our account of Foucault's law and Derrida's description of the relationship of law and justice in his essay, 'Force of Law: The "Mystical Foundation of Authority"', trans. Mary Quaintance, in *Acts of Religion*, ed. Gil Anidjar (New York: Routledge, 2002), pp. 228–98. See the discussion in our Introduction in the text accompanying notes 24–26.
162 Cf. Foucault, *Security, Territory, Population*, p. 46.
163 Michel Foucault, 'The Political Technology of Individuals', in *Essential Works of Foucault, Vol. 3: Power*, pp. 403–17 (p. 417).
164 *Ibid.*, p. 417.
165 Foucault, 'Lemon and Milk', p. 438 (emphasis in original). For a similar distinction, see Michel Foucault, 'The Punitive Society', in *Essential Works of Foucault, Vol. 1: Ethics*, pp. 23–37 (p. 31).
166 Foucault, 'The Political Technology of Individuals', p. 417.
167 Foucault, *Discipline and Punish*, p. 224.
168 Brent L. Pickett, 'Foucaultian Rights?' (2000) 37 *Social Science Journal* 403, 412.
169 Foucault, 'Lemon and Milk', p. 437.
170 *Ibid.*, p. 436.
171 Jean-Luc Nancy, *Being Singular Plural*, trans. Robert D. Richardson and Anne E. O'Byrne (Stanford, CA: Stanford University Press, 2000), p. 131.
172 Giorgio Agamben, *Homo Sacer: Sovereign Power and Bare Life*, trans. Daniel Heller-Roazen (Stanford, CA: Stanford University Press, 1998), p. 52. Agamben evokes a similar law, a law of 'absolute mutability', in his discussion of the Torah as an incoherent medley of meaningless letters (see Giorgio Agamben, 'The Messiah and the Sovereign: The Problem of Law in Walter Benjamin', in *Potentialities: Collected Essays in Philosophy*, trans. Daniel Heller-Roazen (Stanford, CA: Stanford University Press, 1999), pp. 160–74 (pp. 164–66).
173 Jacques Derrida, 'Before the Law', trans. Avital Ronnel (amended and updated by Christine Roulston), in *Acts of Literature*, ed. Derek Attridge (New York and London: Routledge, 1992), pp. 181–220 (p. 190).
174 *Ibid.*, p. 191 (emphasis in original).
175 Bob Fine, *Democracy and the Rule of Law: Liberal Ideals and Marxist Critiques* (London and Sydney: Pluto Press, 1984), p. 200.
176 Foucault, *Discipline and Punish*, pp. 87, 178.
177 Foucault, 'Maurice Blanchot: The Thought from Outside', p. 35.
178 *Ibid.*, p. 35. Here, and elsewhere in the piece, such as on p. 33, where he writes that 'the presence of the law is its concealment', and on pp. 36–37, where he writes that 'the law itself ... is manifested in its essential

concealment', Foucault mirrors some of the terminology of Derrida in 'Before the Law'. For example, see Derrida's statement that the 'law', in Kafka's parable, 'manifests itself in its non-manifestation'. Derrida, 'Before the Law', p. 206.

179 Foucault, 'Nietzsche, Genealogy, History', p. 378.
180 Foucault, *The History of Sexuality, Vol. 1*, p. 87.
181 Foucault, *Security, Territory, Population*, p. 99.
182 Foucault, *The History of Sexuality, Vol. 1*, p. 144.
183 Foucault, *Discipline and Punish*, p. 47. Whilst the 'expulsion thesis' focuses upon Foucault's descriptions of modernity as evidencing the claim that law has become marginalized or subordinated in his work, we include references here to pre-modern instances of law's instrumental subordination to power in Foucault's account so as to show that Foucault saw law as always having been instrumentalized.
184 *Ibid.*, p. 50.
185 *Ibid.*, p. 50.
186 *Ibid.*, p. 22.
187 Foucault, *The History of Sexuality, Vol. 1*, p. 144. The original French passage reads: '[l]a loi ne peut pas ne pas être armée, et son arme, par excellence, c'est la mort' (Michel Foucault, *La volonté de savoir* (Paris: Gallimard, 1976), p. 189). We would translate this passage as follows: 'the law cannot help but be armed, and its weapon, *par excellence*, is death'. In relation to modern law at least, we would dissent from Foucault to the extent that he argues here that death is necessarily the weapon *par excellence* of the law – for us, death represents the very limit of the law, a failure and denial of law's responsive dimension. For Foucault's more nuanced discussions of the effect of the death penalty on a system of penal justice, and on his rejection of 'definitive punishment' without recourse or revision, see Michel Foucault, 'Against Replacement Penalties', in *Essential Works of Foucault, Vol. 3: Power*, pp. 459–61. See also Michel Foucault, 'Pompidou's Two Deaths' and 'To Punish Is the Most Difficult Thing There Is', both reproduced in *Essential Works of Foucault, Vol. 3: Power*, at pp. 418–22 and 462–64.
188 Foucault, *The History of Sexuality, Vol. 1*, p. 144.
189 Foucault, *Discipline and Punish*, p. 98.
190 *Ibid.*, p. 19.
191 *Ibid.*, p. 170.
192 Foucault, *'Society Must Be Defended'*, pp. 38–39.
193 Foucault, 'What is Called "Punishing"?', p. 389. See also Michel Foucault, 'About the Concept of the "Dangerous Individual" in Nineteenth-Century Legal Psychiatry', in *Essential Works of Foucault, Vol. 3: Power*, pp. 176–200 (p. 179, although for a contrary formulation see p. 200).
194 Barron, 'Legal Discourse and the Colonisation of the Self in the Modern State', p. 118.
195 Foucault, 'Lemon and Milk', p. 436.
196 *Ibid.*, p. 436.
197 *Ibid.*, p. 436.
198 Foucault, quoted in Colin Gordon, 'Governmental Rationality: An Introduction', in *The Foucault Effect*, pp. 1–51 (p. 5).
199 Foucault, *Discipline and Punish*, p. 223.

200 Foucault, 'Nietzsche, Genealogy, History', p. 378.
201 Foucault, 'Powers and Strategies', p. 141.
202 Foucault, 'What is Critique?', p. 383. The quotation here refers to Foucault's conception of critique but we are borrowing it in order to describe law in this context, and in the next chapter we shall seek to repay this loan by demonstrating affinities between Foucault's conception of law and his conception of critique.

Chapter 3

Futures of law

He is a nomad, even in his work: do you believe that he has built his house? Not at all. 'That's not it', he said to me about his last volume, 'I've been mistaken. I have to re-cast everything. Go elsewhere. Do it otherwise'.[1]

Any account of a thought rendered in terms of its being unfinished, uncontainable, illimitable, and so forth, ultimately finds itself at the end of a discussion such as the present one in the somewhat unenviable position of nevertheless having to account, of having to conclude in some putatively 'final' way, resolving that which resists resolution. The predictable expedient adopted for refusing this exigency here, given the thematic of generative *ir*resolution that we introduced in the previous chapter, is to 'conclude' not by way of summation but in fact by seeking to push Foucault's thoughts on law further. So far, our discussion of Foucault's law in this book has followed a fairly well rehearsed academic script in which we have sought to disturb the settled scene of standard interpretations and to install a new interpretation in its place. Having surveyed the extant perspectives in Chapter 1 and having then outlined our refinement and (in places) reversal of these perspectives in Chapter 2, we want now in this final chapter to extend our own claims for Foucault's law. This involves us not so much in 'correcting' or 'completing' Foucault, as an ascendant revisionism would have it,[2] but rather in developing his thought along certain lines which he himself neither fully explored nor explicitly thematized in the way in which we do here (but which lines are, as we shall demonstrate, consonant with the interpretation we have developed in the previous chapters).[3] In thus developing Foucault we take our cue from Foucault himself, for, as he famously said of one of his own more salient intellectual forebears, Friedrich Nietzsche, '[t]he only valid tribute to thought such as Nietzsche's is precisely to use it, to make it groan and protest'.[4] Our aim in this chapter, then, will be to use Foucault's late reflections on ethics and critical ontology in order to expand upon the thematic introduced briefly at the conclusion of the last chapter: namely, the idea of law's futurity.[5] This is the idea of law providing the means for a future of our being-together in and as society. What we want to show in this chapter is precisely how law, through its responsive orientation to the ultimate contingency and unpredictability of the future, is a constituent component of the social bond in modernity. As our argument develops, we shall try to show that – far from law being relegated or expelled in modernity – Foucault's aleatory law in fact comes to generate our conjoint and continuate existence in and as society. This law of our being-together, this law of sociality, is the law of Foucault's law. However, before we outline the particular contours of our reading in this chapter let us first take stock of how our argument has developed up to this point.

Chapter 1 presented a synoptic version of the prevailing 'expulsion thesis', in which Foucault is said to have made law instrumentally dependent upon, and subordinated to, the new power formations of modernity, thus denigrating and 'expelling' the law and denying it any constitutive role within that modernity. Against this interpretation the contending readings that we surveyed all tried to embed the law within, or to articulate it with, Foucault's concepts of disciplinary power and governmentality – the aim being to demonstrate that law remained in place in Foucault's modernity (either as an accomplice of disciplinary power or as a technology of government, for example). As we indicated, our reservations about these counter-readings of Foucault on law were simply that they failed fully to capture the specificity of law, or to render an account of law's different constituent dimensions. Drawing upon and yet departing from these readings, we presented our interpretation of Foucault's law in Chapter 2. We first demonstrated how Foucault's law could not be subordinated to, or surpassed by, disciplinary power because in Foucault's work law exists in a relational dynamic of mutual constitution with disciplinary power. In this light, disciplinary power was revealed to be, all along, constituently dependent upon law. We then moved from the failure of disciplinary power to be comprehensively coherent to the generative incoherence of Foucault's law itself. In our reading, Foucault's law is a vacuous law which in its very penetration by powers outside or beyond it nevertheless holds itself ultimately resistant to, and uncontainable by, those same powers. Whilst Foucault's law was instrumentally subordinated to the dictates of disciplinary power, bio-power, and diverse agents and sites of governmentality, we nevertheless tried to show how it is that the very quality of openness or responsiveness which allows law to be subordinated in this way also guarantees that it cannot ever be definitively encompassed by any external or putatively superordinate power.

Contrary to received renditions of his views on law, then, the trend of our argument thus far has been that Foucault does not in fact relegate or 'expel' the law but rather gives us a law which, in its ever becoming other than what it is, avoids encapsulation by power. What we now want to do is to press Foucault's thought and to show how, through his later discussions of ethics and critical ontology, we can derive an understanding of this same law, one which places it at the very centre of the social bond in modernity. This social bond is not, however, the comfortable enclosure and sheltering of a *socius* but rather the dispersal and the suscitating opening of society to alterity (or, as Foucault pithily proclaims in *The Archaeology of Knowledge*, 'we are difference ... [and such difference is] this dispersion that we are and make').[6] In short, we argue in this chapter that Foucault's law, in its responsive openness, provides a constituent condition of our being-together in and as society. The basic argument which will now be elaborated is to the effect that any society, or political formation, must, in order to continue in being, have some constituent regard to futurity. Such an attunement or orientation to futurity imports both an incorporative engagement with the future which attempts to make determinate provision in the existent for what the future brings, but also an unconditional openness to what in the future remains irreducibly to come, with the wholly other. Indeed, futurity in this latter sense impinges upon and radically disrupts the self-presence of the present, which cannot 'be' on its own, without a past and a future that is always coming. We have seen already in Chapter 2 that the key to law's futurity, to the endurance of law, is its very responsive openness. What we are seeking to do in this chapter now is to connect that very quality of law – which is, we argue, *the* abiding quality of law, that by which law abides – with questions of social organization and the social bond. Our argument is that law is a constituent source of our continuate being-together, and it is precisely through its responsiveness that it achieves this.

In this final chapter, we set our account of the sociality of Foucault's law within the context of two opposed figurations of the political formation of modernity which we derive from Foucault's work. These two different figurations of Occidental political modernity represent answers, or responses, as it were, to the question of social organization. Foucault broaches this question in the piece we discussed towards the end of the previous chapter, 'A Preface to Transgression',[7] describing the emergence of modernity in familiarly Nietzschean terms as an event precipitated by the death of God.[8] This modernity, Foucault tells us, is a 'world now emptied of objects, beings, and spaces to desecrate' and one which consequently 'no longer recognizes any positive meaning in the sacred'.[9] In contrast to a stilled pre-modernity of myth, symbol and religion, this profane modernity eschews constituent reliance upon a world apart from itself and, following the inaugurating deicide, there can be no resort to transcendental references such as God in order to ground authority or guarantee meaning. Consequently, in the 'ontological void'[10] of modernity we are ever consigned 'to a world exposed by the experience of its limits, made and unmade by that excess which transgresses it'.[11] Meaning unmoored, this restless modernity is a 'scintillating and constantly affirmed world'[12] in which, bereft of sacral fixity, we must negotiate 'in an uncertain context, in certainties ... immediately upset'.[13] Without deific or transcendent grounds for our modern being, Foucault tells us, we are consigned to a modernity that is a 'world exposed'.[14] How does one relate to others in such an exposed modernity? How might one grasp an attenuate stability or a sense of being-in-common in a world in constituent flux, of things falling apart, centres not holding and prior solidities melting importunately into air?[15] What permanence or perdurance can be achieved? And what does such a situation import for law?

Foucault then presents two antinomic, yet integrally related, responses to the question of social organization in modernity: simply, modernity as *closure* and modernity as *rupture*. In his work, we see a split between a (familiar) modernity in which all is disciplined into place, and a modernity of rupture, transgression and distanciation. In this latter guise, being (or, perhaps more appositely, becoming) modern imports a willingness to transgress one's limits in the direction of an as-yet-unimagined and unimaginable future, with new ways of being, of being otherwise. In the ensuing two sections of this chapter we discuss two different models of legality which correspond to these two aspects, or opposed imperatives, of the political formation of modernity. The first response, represented by the jurisprudential writings of Foucault's former colleague François Ewald on the theme of 'social law', attempts to constrict society by proposing means by which society can coincide with itself. It is a legality of compromise and circumscription, a legality of normalization and settlement. What we will ultimately seek to show is how this response of legal closure and a securing of determinate limits actually provokes and necessitates (following the mobile 'logic' of Foucault's law which we outlined in the previous chapter) a counter-response. This second response is the one we develop at greater length here, and is based upon Foucault's late reflections on ethics and critical ontology. Such a response represents a more labile and adaptive legality which, in its enduring responsiveness to that which is to come, is commensurate with Foucault's evocation of a futural modernity, of a being beyond oneself. In this final chapter, then, we want to push Foucault's thoughts on law further and in so doing to connect them with a thinking of sociality and social organization. We start with Ewald's legal closure of the social.

EWALD AND THE MODERNIST CLOSURE OF THE SOCIAL

The question of the political formations of modernity is a recurrent one in Foucault's thought, and one which receives – as we have indicated above – somewhat different formulations. The more remarked upon formulation of modernity in Foucault's political thought is of modernity as a time of closure, a denial of possibility and alterity. This is the first response to modernity we touched on briefly in the preceding paragraph. Perhaps most (in)famously, Foucault depicted modernity – largely in works such as *Discipline and Punish* and his interventions into political theory in the mid-1970s – not as a time of autonomy, self-discovery and liberation but rather as the moment when the knowledges of man deployed in the human sciences saw the strict disciplining of time and space in increasing areas of institutional and social life, and populations became subject to ever-increasing regulatory control. As Douglas Litowitz has it, Foucault's modernity emerges as a 'negative utopia' of Orwellian dimensions.[16] It is indeed this aspect of Foucault's description of modernity that has attracted most criticism from the philosophical inheritors and proponents of the Enlightenment legacy. They would charge Foucault with having painted a bleakly dystopic and claustrophobic picture of modernity as a prison house from which there is no possibility of escape.[17] Modernity in this guise effects, or tries to effect, a disciplining reduction to the norm. It is this aspect of the political formation of modernity which we ultimately see reflected in the jurisprudential writings of an important legal philosopher whose work we encountered towards the end of Chapter 1: François Ewald.

In sketching the first of two possible modern legalities, two possible socialities of law, we want now to return in more detail to the writings of Ewald. Ewald has developed a series of Foucaultian reflections on the themes of 'social law' and 'the law of law',[18] and in bringing a Foucaultian perspective to bear upon the question of law's relation to social organization has eloquently attested to one dimension of this problem. As we shall see, Ewald's particular articulation of the law of the law, or the sociality of law, is oriented towards the setting of determinate limits to the social space of modernity. In what follows, we shall see how the figure of Ewald's 'social law' appears as the guarantee of the closure – or, in Ewald's Foucaultian-inflected terms, the *normalization* – of the conflictual space of sociality, and how without more (that is, without an attunement to the 'more' that exceeds any instantiation of the social and which is always and utterly beyond compromise and circumscription), it fails to offer the constituent possibility of a social always open to alterity, of a social beyond itself, of different modalities of our being-together. Let us first address Ewald's conception of the law of the law, before beginning to articulate our responsive alternative and supplement in the ensuing section.

Ewald starts his account of the law of the law with a statement of fact and necessity: 'It is a fact that there is no (positive) law without a law of law; no law without a principle, an instance of reflexion, whereby the law thinks about itself.'[19] This principle is formulated later in the same piece as the *rule of judgement*:

> To describe the element of reflexivity of law, I propose to speak of a *rule of judgement*. Legislation, doctrine and case law are all practices of legal judgement. Their articulation, distribution and mutual competence depend on the type of rationality that this legal judgement obeys. This type of rationality defines, for a particular legal order, the economy of its 'juris-diction'. The rule of judgement is not a rule laid down by a body, but is what regulates the judgement of all bodies; accordingly, not something that one applies, but something whereby one judges.[20]

Now, classical accounts of a rule of judgement or a law of the law render it as a constituent source of law set compendiously apart from the profane world – as the divine order of the cosmos, the word of God, or natural law, for example. Ewald sets his account of the modern social logic of the law, of the law of modern law, in a world bereft of such resorts – natural law and other such comforting verities are no longer epistemologically available for us. We moderns, for whom 'the idea of natural law ... has become alien', cannot ground our law in such sources.[21] 'It is typical of present-day legal experience', writes Ewald, 'that the idea of natural law has become impossible ... for us.'[22] Indeed, he tells us, such a loss 'marks the legal experience's entry into the age of modernity'.[23]

This modernist return to earth brings with it an embrace of the social as the constitutive source of legality. 'The law was henceforth to be social',[24] remarks Ewald of the late nineteenth-century critique of *jusnaturalism*. When, in modernity, law 'cannot [found itself upon] ... a doctrine of natural law', then, Ewald notes, we are faced with the task of constructing a 'law of law, which must itself be social'.[25] Modern law thus finds its ultimate support in its 'contact' with sociality. Ewald writes thus: 'It would no doubt be truer to say that the rule of judgment is that whereby a legal system closed round its own order comes into contact with its exterior: what one in general calls the social.'[26] Ewald's conception of the social rehearses and relies upon standard tropes we have encountered above. The 'social space' is 'animated by perpetual movement' and the 'social bond' is thus of necessity 'continually nego-tiated and renegotiated'.[27] Ewald's social is a space of 'dispersion',[28] a 'conflictual, divided vision' of clashing interests,[29] and in this he is no doubt close to the Foucault of *'Society Must Be Defended'*, for whom the model of war provided an apt grid of intelligibility to decipher the space of the social.[30] And yet given this formulation of the lability of the social, of its movement and chance discontinuity from itself, it is some-what surprising that the sociality which Ewald invokes as the constituent sociality of law is ultimately set in its positivity and self-enclosure. And what is more it is the social law, a law of normality, that for him orchestrates this very closure.

How can Ewald's conflictual sociality ultimately resolve itself into a positivity? For Ewald, as we have seen, modern law finds its ground in the social. In this way, Ewald sets his notion of a modern social law against a Kantian understanding of law, 'namely a set of rational state-ments which, detached from desires, interests, and passions – even moral ones – might be the foundation for an order of coexistence of liber-ties'.[31] *Contra* Kant, the foundation of Ewald's social law is in its being a part of the social contest, not in its putatively objective detachment from it: 'Social law is seen as an [*sic*] political instrument, as an instrument of government.'[32] It seeks to be 'an instrument of intervention which is to serve to compensate [for] and correct inequalities, to restore threatened equilibria'.[33] Ewald's social law avowedly enters the social fray, as an instrument of settlement, balance and compromise of the conflictual interests which go to constitute the social. 'The law is no longer a factor external to the conflict whereby it may be resolved',[34] but, on the con-trary, law's being social consists of, and requires, its integration into and management of social strife:

> The law no longer conceals that it is at once the effect and the prize of particular interests in conflict. Its value is no longer related so much to its constitutional status as to its technical advantages as an instrument for the sociological administration of society.[35]

Modern law, on Ewald's account, does not stand apart from or above society in its aloof generality or abstraction but rather constitutes a particular instrument for facilitating the 'compromise' between parts of that society, and indeed ultimately the 'coincidence' of that society with itself.[36] The instrumentality of law is a weapon in the mediation of a conflictual social space:

> From collective bargaining to mediation, there is a whole range of practices aimed at allowing 'society' continually to reach a compromise with itself, to bring forth its own law, its own normativity. These practices, made compulsory in a law of settlements, bring along the dream of a self-managing society.[37]

For Ewald, '[o]ne term sums up the whole set of characteristics of this logic of legal judgment: the term *norm*'.[38] The norm is not related to a 'fixed, transcendent measure'[39] but is, as the above quotation intimates, derived from society itself. The norm in its embeddedness and its social positivity manages miraculously to fuse fact and value (it compendiously designates 'both what the social logic is and what it ought to be'),[40] and it is indeed '[t]hanks to the norm … [that] "society" will be able to judge itself in continual adjustment to itself, which is what the social lawyers have been claiming as the ideal to aim at'.[41] The norm, as a 'pure instrument of comparison', provides a 'regular statement of society's relationship with itself'.[42] As such, and for Ewald, it provides a 'principle of justice'[43] – in fact, he emphasizes that '[s]ocial justice is a justice of the norm'.[44] This means, ultimately, that for Ewald 'the norm is the modern form of the social bond',[45] for justice – a specifically *social* justice, that is – inheres in the ability of society, through the 'imaginary point' of the norm, to 'see itself as one'.[46]

Let us briefly summarize Ewald's position before outlining an alternative notion of the law of the law as the law of the social bond – a social bond that does not subsist in replete coherence and reference to itself but rather in its very dissolution and disjunction from itself. For Ewald, then, modern law must needs renounce reliance on natural or God-given premises. The epistemological unavailability of these atavistic resorts in modernity leads to law founding itself upon sociality. However, the sociality that law, founded now upon the norm, brings to bear and which supposedly carries its being in modernity is a sociality of balance and compromise, and one which aims at permanence and coherence:

> The societies of solidarity have their coherence assured by economic and sociological positivities. … The norm defines the conditions of

what takes the place of the social contract in the solidarity societies: *consensus*. It is both the reference and the object of consensus. It indicates the price to be paid for the advantages of solidarity; it allows the cost-benefit balance sheet of belonging to society to be drawn up. The norm serves as a reference for a negotiation which it makes permanent. It is also the thing the negotiation has to correct. ... The norm is the rule of judgement that allows objectivity of judgement of oneself by oneself – a specifically social objectivity.[47]

Ewald's law of modern law is thus the law of calibrated consensus – the result of a cost-benefit analysis conducted by and in the name of a 'society' which can in its confident self-reference comprise and judge its own normality.[48] This sociality, we argue, reflects Foucault's formulation of modernity as *closure*, as a normalizing constriction and attempt to determine the range of relation and being. But Foucault, as we intimated above, also conceived of modernity in very different terms, and it is in these terms that we now introduce an alternative to Ewald's thinking of law as social closure.

THE MODERNITY OF FOUCAULTIAN ETHICS

In a late text called 'What is Enlightenment?', Foucault strikingly defines modernity as an *attitude* that one adopts towards the present:

> I know that modernity is often spoken of as an epoch, or at least as a set of features characteristic of an epoch; situated on a calendar, it would be preceded by a more or less naive or archaic premodernity, and followed by an enigmatic and troubling 'postmodernity'. ... I wonder whether we may not envisage modernity as an attitude rather than as a period of history.[49]

Somewhat surprisingly given his previous assessments of him, the exemplar of this modern attitude turns out to be Immanuel Kant.[50] The first half of Foucault's text is a reading of Kant's famous response of November 1784 to the *Berlinische Monatschrift*: 'An Answer to the Question: "What is Enlightenment?"'[51] According to Foucault, Kant's discussion of Enlightenment was:

> [T]he first time that a philosopher [had] connected in this way, closely and from the inside, the significance of his work with respect to knowledge [*connaissance*], a reflection on history and a particular

analysis of the specific moment at which he is writing and because of which he is writing. It is in the reflection on 'today' as difference in history and as motive for a particular philosophical task that the novelty of this text appears to me to lie. And, by looking at it in this way, it seems to me we may recognize a point of departure: the outline of what one might call the attitude of modernity.[52]

What does this 'attitude of modernity' entail? 'For the attitude of modernity', Foucault explains, 'the high value of the present is indissociable from a desperate eagerness to imagine it, to imagine it otherwise than it is.'[53] This modern attitude, this 'entire form of philosophical reflection',[54] thus requires simultaneously a 'permanent critique of ourselves'[55] and a 'permanent creation of ourselves':[56]

> I shall thus characterize the philosophical ethos appropriate to the critical ontology of ourselves as a historico-practical test of the limits we may go beyond, and thus as work carried out by ourselves upon ourselves as free beings.[57]

Foucault writes of his notion of critique that:

> This philosophical ethos may be characterized as a *limit-attitude*. We are not talking about a gesture of rejection. We have to move beyond the outside-inside alternative; we have to be at the frontiers. Criticism indeed consists of analyzing and reflecting upon limits. But if the Kantian question was that of knowing [*savoir*] what limits knowledge [*connaissance*] must renounce exceeding, it seems to me that the critical question today must be turned back into a positive one. ... The point, in brief, is to transform the critique conducted in the form of necessary limitation into a practical critique that takes the form of a possible crossing-over [*franchissement*].[58]

This crossing-over of limits is integral to the experience of modernity and to the 'critical interrogation on the present and on ourselves'[59] which modernity requires. Thus, finally:

> The critical ontology of ourselves must be considered not, certainly, as a theory, a doctrine, nor even as a permanent body of knowledge that is accumulating; it must be conceived as an attitude, an ethos, a philosophical life in which the critique of what we are is at one and the same time the historical analysis of the limits imposed on

us and an experiment with the possibility of going beyond them [*de leur franchissement possible*].[60]

In these formulations Foucault describes an opposed understanding of modernity – modernity now emerges as an attitude which one adopts towards the present, an attitude which enjoins what Foucault calls a 'critical ontology' towards one's being, and, as we shall soon see, one's being-in-common or one's being-together with others. This is modernity as constituent lability and contestation, and modernity as *rupture*. This formulation of modernity provides means of thinking the sociality of law in modernity going beyond Ewald's notion of law as social closure. If for Ewald the movement of justice is in the direction of the cohering of the social (hence his specific articulation of 'social justice'), then for us – following our discussion of Foucault's law in Chapter 2 – the direction of justice is in the reverse direction. It is in the responsive dimension of Foucault's law, in its ever incorporatively engaging with its outside and in its undoing of its determinate self in the process, that we locate the sociality and the (ever unattainable) justice of law.

What we seek to describe here is a constituent sociality of law, but this sociality is not an enfolding within but rather the unworking of the space of the social – a thinking of *dissensus* as opposed to *consensus*. The law of the law in modernity thus resides in law's responsive dimension, in its being able to open society to alterity, to an ethic of constantly being otherwise. Foucault's law, as we have described it in the preceding chapter, is the medium of this unsettled exchange, the constituent condition of our being-together, where this being-together cannot be reduced to a justice of enclosure and the immanent regularities of the social. If for Ewald 'the very question of justice' is the problem of the incommensurability of 'one man ... with another', a question to which the norm (as a 'principle of commensurability') furnishes a ready answer, then it is precisely this answer which for us Foucault is concerned to reject.[61] For Foucault, importantly, such a principle of social commensurability could never 'work' or assume any enduring existence. Recalling our discussion in Chapter 2 of the way in which modern law, through its articulation with disciplinary power, attempted to ground itself in the factuality of the human and the normative determinations of the human sciences (as Foucault puts it in *Discipline and Punish*, 'law must appear to be a necessity of things'[62] or be 'grounded in truth'[63]), we saw how this project of social comprehension and accounting was doomed to failure. Borrowing the thought from Claude Lefort, such a project was always mired in 'illusion'.[64] The social cannot, through the medium of the norm, 'account for itself'.[65]

More crucially, though, Foucault would locate the possibility and the promise of sociability not in modes of social accounting or rendering oneself normal, but in getting afield of and exceeding such stultifying and cohesive normality – that is, precisely, in a resistance to the norm. For Foucault, especially in his late work on ethics and critical ontology, sociability inheres in transgressing the *socius* and its constraints, in pluralizing relations and multiplying affects beyond range of the norm. As Paul Rabinow notes in his 'Introduction' to the first volume of Foucault's *Essential Works*, Foucault's late work centres upon the transformative value and function of thought for the knower who, in the process of thinking, 'stray[s] afield from himself'.[66] As Rabinow goes on to point out, the French word that Foucault uses in the above piece and which is translated as 'straying afield of oneself' is *égarement*, which Rabinow proceeds to define, citing *Le Robert* dictionary, as 'an action of getting a distance from what is defined as morality, reason, and the norm, and the state that ensues'.[67] As François Delaporte puts it in relation to Canguilhem, Foucault's tutor on the norm, '[w]e must move, err, adapt to survive. This condition of "erring or drifting" is not merely accidental or external to life but its fundamental form.'[68] In short, then, a generative erring from the norm, a critical distancing of oneself from the conditioned norm. It is in the opening of this errant critical distance, in the 'straying afield of' the determinate limits of what is normal and what is social, that Foucault finds the very promise of sociability, the promise of other forms of our being-together.

So, to recap, Foucault depicts modernity not simply as constraint and closure but also characterizes it as the experience of a restless crossing-over, of an insistent and unremitting transgression of boundaries of identity and community. For law to be commensurate with this futural and ruptural experience of modernity it must be able both to enforce a delimitable presence and, more crucially (as we stressed in Chapter 2), to respond adaptively, envisioning other modes and ways of being. Indeed, as we also saw in Chapter 2 in discussing Foucault's engagements with the thought of Georges Bataille and Maurice Blanchot, law is itself formed in and through the very contestation of its determinant position. It is this movement, the movement of exteriority, which is constitutive of Foucault's law. This law of being otherwise is the very law of the law, and it is in this that law's sociability consists. This responsive quality of law means that it can serve as the constituent source of our sociality, of our being-together. Law does not, nor can it, simply attain a positive 'social justice' through a gathering and sheltering of the *socius* (per Ewald). This, without more, would in fact be a denial of any possibility of sociability, of different ways of being and of relating to each other – such would be an improvident legality, set in its forestalling of futurity. Rather, law in its responsive dimension is the means by which concrete instantiations of the *socius* can be amenably interrupted and unmade, reiterated and made anew, even entirely anew. It is in this suscitating ability to form and iteratively re-form the social bond, to both provide the delimitation of a given society or community and through its vacating of that content to provide an opening for its being ever otherwise, that law finds the law of its existence. In the following comments we illustrate how these qualities of law are reflected in Foucault's late account of ethics and critical ontology. Indeed, we argue that in these formulations Foucault is in fact offering us several different components of the law of the law in modernity. It may at first sight seem strange to locate resonances with modernity in Foucault's return to Greece but, as we seek to demonstrate, Foucault's engagement with antiquity is impelled by the political imperatives of the present (and, more appositely perhaps, the imperative of politically contesting the present). We now turn to engage with Foucault's ethics.

Foucault's ethics is most fully articulated in the second and third volumes of the *History of Sexuality* project, published in 1984 (*The Use of Pleasure* and *The Care of the Self*, respectively).[69] This engagement with ethics arises at the end of a conceptual trajectory in which Foucault moves from a predominant concern with the way in which individuals are objectified within regimes of power (as detailed in *Discipline and Punish* and the first volume of *The History of Sexuality*), to an analysis of the way in which subjects are enjoined both to conduct themselves and to conduct others (as discussed in the work on governmentality), and then finally to a concern with the way in which subjects constitute themselves as the ethical subjects of their own actions. Or, as Foucault puts it in a 1982 seminar:

> Perhaps I've insisted too much on the technology of domination and power. I am more and more interested in the interaction between oneself and others, and in the technologies of individual domination, in the mode of action that an individual exercises upon himself by means of the technologies of the self.[70]

As we shall see, the emphasis in Foucault's late writings on technologies of the self is increasingly placed not so much on the ways in which individuals dominate themselves by way of such modalities as 'governing through freedom', 'responsibilization' and 'government-at-a-distance' found in much of the literature on governmentality,[71] but rather on the creative, self-constitutive possibilities of these technologies. Importantly, we read this development in Foucault's late work (and the conception of subjectivity which it imports) as a change of emphasis, as a 'modification' of his previous conceptions and not as a radical departure from, or a major revision of, them.[72] And, as is now well known, in order to derive a model for a constituent mode of acting upon oneself (which Foucault calls ethics), he leaves the more familiar territory of modernity and returns to the sources of classical Greek and imperial Roman antiquity.

In the ensuing discussion, however, we shall try to demonstrate that these antique sources actually provide Foucault with the very model of a modern ethical project – an ethical project which comports with that understanding of modernity instanced above, a modernity of rupture, contestation and becoming. In the pages that follow, we engage at some length with Foucault's understanding of ethics. We begin by giving a description of what Foucault means by ethics in the late work before pursuing our argument that in this late work on ethics Foucault is not trying to recuperate some inner, subjective experience but is in fact articulating a form of *sociality*. This sociality provides a model for law's sociality, a sociality in which we are constantly enjoined to (re)negotiate our limits and to have a responsive regard to futurity and to the inventions of alterity. Let us first describe the contours of Foucault's ethics before expanding upon our argument and then relating it to law, but it will be as well to keep in mind that the purpose of our engagement throughout is to demonstrate the *sociality* of Foucault's ethical project.

In an interview with Hubert Dreyfus and Paul Rabinow, 'On the Genealogy of Ethics: An Overview of Work in Progress', Foucault summarizes the understanding of ancient Greek ethics that he develops in the second and third volumes of the *History of Sexuality* project. In the following excerpt from the interview he explains the relationship which existed at the time between morality and ethics, and it is a useful synoptic overview of what he derives from the ancient Greeks:

> I think, in general, we have to distinguish, where the history of morals is concerned, acts and moral code. The acts (*conduites*) are the real behavior of people in relation to the moral code (*prescriptions*) which are [*sic*] imposed on them. I think we have to distinguish between the code which determines which acts are permitted or forbidden and the code which determines the positive or negative value of the different possible behaviors – you're not allowed to have sex with anyone but your wife, that's an element of the code. And there is another side to the moral prescriptions, which most of the time is not isolated as such but is, I think, very important: the kind of relationship you

ought to have with yourself, *rapport à soi*, which I call ethics, and which determines how the individual is supposed to constitute himself as a moral subject of his own actions.[73]

In the same interview, Foucault goes on to subdivide the properly ethical domain of the relationship to oneself, the *rapport à soi*, into four separate elements.[74] There is first of all the *ethical substance*. The ethical substance is that part of the ethical subject's behaviour which is to be problematized and made the subject of ethical reflection and elaboration. For example, this could be one's dietary intake, one's physical appearance, or one's sexual behaviour. In his study of the ethics of the ancient Greeks in *The Use of Pleasure* Foucault found that the subject of ethical reflection was the *aphrodisia*, or the configuration of 'acts linked to pleasure and desire in their unity' (not to be confused with later Christian notions of the flesh or modern understandings of sexuality).[75] Secondly, there is the *mode of subjection or subjectivation*. The mode of subjection is the manner in which 'people are invited or incited to recognize their moral obligations'.[76] This could be through a recognition of divine law, or scripture, or some secular commandment. Thirdly, there is the element of *asceticism*. As we shall see below, Foucault's usage of asceticism differs markedly from Christian meanings with their connotations of self-renunciation and abnegation – asceticism in Foucault's reading of the Greeks is not primarily a self-renunciating or mortificatory practice but is in fact a 'self-forming activity'.[77] What Foucault intends by asceticism here is really a mode of working upon oneself, or, rather, upon the ethical substance. This practice could involve a dietary regime, a program of bodily training, or a practice of writing or stylizing the self (perhaps through the use of diaries or other media). Finally, there is the *telos*, or goal, of this ethical self-elaboration. In applying the arts of ascecis to those parts of our selves which are in need of elaboration or improvement, do we aim thereby to achieve self-mastery, purity, an ideal of beauty, or some other goal? In summary, then, Foucault's reading of ancient Greek ethics locates ethics as a subset of a larger domain of morality. What is definitive about ethics, on this view, is neither the ethical subject's relationship to the moral code (as we might find in Kantian formulations, for example) nor his relationship to another who is to be accorded some kind of ontological-ethical priority (as we might find in Levinasian formulations, for example).[78] Rather, the priority in Foucault's reading of ancient Greek ethics is the self's relationship to itself, as practised through a series of ascetic technologies which aim to elaborate, improve and re-form the self along certain lines in order to attain a certain state of being. Foucaultian ethics, as derived from the ancients, is hence best understood as an *ethos*, as a way of being and acting. Foucault's late work has been characterized in two related, yet somewhat misleading, ways. The first is that in his formulation of ethics Foucault reintroduces a liberal subject – an essentialized, metaphysical *subjectum* somehow 'beyond power and knowledge'.[79] The second characterization is that even if Foucault does not succumb to the temptations of metaphysics, the technology of ethical self-constitution which he advocates leads to a subjectivity turned in upon itself. The late Foucaultian subject, so goes this reading, simply seeks to confirm itself in its own sovereign self-mastery and possession and has no regard for alterity. Our argument with respect to both characterizations will be that Foucault is neither reliant upon unarticulated metaphysical presuppositions nor is his figure of ethical subjectivity a form of self-enclosure, but rather that in and through his late ethics Foucault thematizes a subject in the world constituently attuned to alterity, one constituted by its engagements with others. Let us deal now with the first criticism, namely that Foucault reintroduces a metaphysical subject into his late work on ethics, saving the second criticism for a discussion later in the chapter.

The first characterization of Foucault's ethics depends upon a reading of the late work as constituting something of a Damascene self-correction. If like Peter Dews we read Foucault as having insisted in the preceding years on the premise that 'subjects are entirely constituted by the operation of power', then the late work might indeed look like an 'abrupt theoretical shift' introduced to mitigate or 'overcome the ambiguity of his earlier relation to concepts of power and emancipation'.[80] As we demonstrated in the last chapter, however, Foucault's previous work on the disciplinary subjection of individuals does *not* imply a subject wholly constituted by the operations of discipline (as Foucault himself insists in a late interview, '[t]he idea that power is a system of domination that controls everything and leaves no room for freedom cannot be attributed to me').[81] Neither, crucially, does Foucault's later work introduce a subject untrammelled by the sedimentations of discourse and power formations. As Foucault puts it in the interview 'The Ethics of the Concern of the Self as a Practice of Freedom':

> I would say that if I am now interested in how the subject constitutes itself in an active fashion through practices of the self, these practices are nevertheless not something invented by the individual. They are models that he finds in his culture and are proposed, suggested, imposed on him by his culture, his society, and his social group.[82]

Indeed, the Foucaultian subject is best understood as 'both crafted and crafting', as something which is enjoined to 'form itself within forms that are already more or less in operation and underway'.[83] The Foucaultian subject is hence not a metaphysical 'substance',[84] but rather the unfinished result of a political negotiation with and through others. Thus, it is crucial to note that Foucault's ethical project is unconcerned with excavating and hence liberating one's true self – this much was evident from Foucault's critique of the 'repressive hypothesis' in the first volume of *The History of Sexuality*.[85] Rather, Foucault's ethical project is in fact deployed *against* those forms of political rationality which aim to define the 'truth' of the subject and to tie the subject to this truth. In the same interview with Dreyfus and Rabinow referenced earlier, Foucault is asked: 'But isn't the Greek concern with the self just an early version of our self-absorption which many consider a central problem in our society?' Foucault's answer is instructive:

> In the California cult of the self, one is supposed to discover one's true self, to separate it from that which might obscure or alienate it, to decipher its truth thanks to psychological or psychoanalytical science, which is supposed to be able to tell you what your true self is. Therefore, not only do I not identify this ancient culture of the self with what you might call the Californian culture of the self, I think they are diametrically opposed.[86]

Foucault here counterposes his ethical vision to a contemporary regime of self-mastery or self-improvement, the Californian cult of the self, but we might add two other negative exemplars which feature repeatedly in Foucault's work: first, the Christian hermeneutic of the self which enjoins a subject to decipher, renounce and obey;[87] and, second, the normalizing knowledge claims of the human sciences which had been the target of so much of Foucault's genealogical analyses of the 1970s.[88] The former hermeneutic is based primarily upon the technique of confession, with its 'indispensable and permanent' obligation to 'seek and state the truth about oneself'.[89] In the Christian hermeneutic there is a constant and inescapable 'spiral' of self-decipherment and self-renunciation such that:

> The more we discover the truth about ourselves, the more we must renounce ourselves; and the more we want to renounce ourselves, the more we need to bring to light the reality of ourselves. That is what we would call the spiral of truth formulation and reality renouncement which is at the heart of Christian techniques of the self.[90]

As Foucault says, this universal hermeneutical obligation of telling the truth about oneself takes the juridical form of a self-incrimination:

> Everyone in Christianity has the duty to explore who he is, what is happening within himself, the faults he may have committed, the temptations to which he is exposed. Moreover, everyone is obliged to tell these things to other people, and thus to bear witness against himself.[91]

And yet whilst this 'permanent hermeneutics of oneself'[92] follows a regime of truth-telling, or veridiction, in which '[s]elf-revelation is at the same time self-destruction',[93] this is not necessarily the case for the modern regime of the human sciences:

> From the eighteenth century to the present, the techniques of verbalization have been reinserted in a different context by the so-called human sciences in order to use them without renunciation of the self but to constitute, positively, a new self. To use these techniques without renouncing oneself constitutes a decisive break.[94]

A decisive break may indeed exist between Christian ascesis and the modern human sciences, but, as Foucault's genealogical work of the mid-1970s makes amply clear, the fabrication of interiority by the modern 'orthopaedists of individuality' and disciplinary experts of the 'psy-' professions was hardly less pernicious in its effect.[95] So, whether Foucault's late ethical project is deployed against the expert rule of those disciplinary scientists who would seek to 'discover' the truth of individuals in order to manipulate them or integrate them into systems of meaning or production, or whether it is directed against more openly theological hermeneutics of the self and their ascetic renunciations, what Foucault is critiquing in both cases is the idea of self-discovery through uncovering one's hidden truth, the essential and unalienated truth of the subject.

Foucault's late work is thus an investigation into the political effects of truth upon the subject and an attempt to articulate a form of resistance to what Foucault calls the 'government of individuals by their own verity'.[96] What are the constraints which result from telling the truth about oneself? What price must the subject pay for telling the truth about him or herself?[97] Ultimately, Foucault's response to the problematic of telling the truth about oneself is to try to rethink the very relation between the subject and truth which is at the heart of both theological and disciplinary modes of subjectivation. Rather than the recovery of the truth of what one is, Foucault argues, we should be attempting instead to create ourselves anew, 'to ... invent', as he says in a late interview, 'a manner of being that is still improbable'.[98] There is thus a refusal of extant forms of subjectivity (a 'desubjectification in the game of what one could call, in a word, the politics of truth')[99] and an injunction to create something entirely different in their place:

> Maybe the target nowadays is not to discover what we are but to refuse what we are. ... We have to promote new forms of subjectivity through the refusal of this kind of individuality which has been imposed on us for several centuries.[100]

Foucault's interest in the ancients' understanding of ethics thus comes from the potential he perceived in the idea of an *ethos* of self-creation to overcome (or at least to modify) some of the political effects of the Christian hermeneutic of confession and the disciplinary normalization of the human sciences (as well as such contemporary manifestations of hermeneutics of the self as the Californian cult of the self, for example). In the late work, Foucault often thematizes this resistant potential, a resistant potential we encountered in the preceding chapter in terms of resistance's *primacy* with respect to power, in terms of *creativity* and *aesthetics*. In discussing how the practitioners of Greek ethics aimed to remake themselves, Foucault places a very heavy emphasis upon the aesthetic dimensions of the project – '[t]he idea of the *bios* as a material for an aesthetic piece of art is something which fascinates me', he readily admitted to his interviewers in 1983.[101] As Foucault explains, 'the principal aim, the principal target of this kind of ethics was an aesthetic one'.[102] The Greeks acted to:

> give to their life certain values (reproduce certain examples, leave behind them an exalted reputation, give the maximum possible brilliance to their lives). It was a question of making one's life into an object for a sort of knowledge, for a *techne* – for an art.[103]

As opposed to Christianity, where 'morality took on increasingly the form of a code of rules', the structure of ethical experience in antiquity was 'elaboration of one's own life as a personal work of art'.[104] This was, and could still be, 'the search for an aesthetics of existence',[105] in which 'we have to create ourselves as a work of art'.[106] References in this context to asceticism and ascetic techniques provide an ironic rejoinder to the Christian connotations of self-denial and abnegation with which the words are heavily freighted today:

Asceticism as the renunciation of pleasure has bad connotations. But ascesis is something else: it's the work that one performs on oneself in order to transform oneself or make the self appear which, happily, one never attains. Can that be our problem today? We've rid ourselves of asceticism.[107]

This ascetic practice constitutes 'an exercise of the self on the self by which one attempts to develop and transform oneself, and to attain a certain mode of being'.[108] And, finally, linking the ascetic with the aesthetic, Foucault observes that '[t]his transformation of one's self by one's own knowledge is, I think, something rather close to the aesthetic experience'.[109] The Foucaultian ethical experience is hence unavoidably an aesthetic-creative one, which poses the multiple truths of the subject as an answer to the hermeneutic injunction to display the unitary, essential truth of what one is.[110]

The earlier reference to the happy fact that one never completely attains one's self aptly reveals that for Foucault the purpose of this aesthetic-ethical work upon oneself is neither to retrieve a lost or authentic sense of self nor to arrive at a final destination – references to art and *techne* are hence perhaps better understood as an ongoing *travail* rather than a completed *oeuvre*. Throughout Foucault's ethical discussions there is a repeated emphasis upon the notion of 'becoming' oneself. This is perhaps most evident in some of Foucault's interventions into debates around gay identity politics in interviews which he gave to the gay press in the late 1970s and early 1980s. These interventions are some of the clearest examples of how Foucault sought to redeploy in a contemporary context the classical ethical notions of working upon oneself and re-recreating oneself anew.[111] For example, in an interview given in 1981 to the French magazine, *Gai Pied*, Foucault observed:

Another thing to distrust is the tendency to relate the question of homosexuality to the problem of 'Who am I?' and 'What is the secret of my desire?' … The problem is not to discover in oneself the truth of one's sex, but, rather, to use one's sexuality henceforth to arrive at a multiplicity of relationships. And, no doubt, that's the real reason why homosexuality is not a form of desire but something desirable. Therefore, we have to work at becoming homosexuals and not be obstinate in recognizing that we are.[112]

In the same interview he remarked on the importance of developing a gay ethics, a gay style and way of life outside existing institutions:

A way of life can be shared among individuals of different age, status, and social activity. It can yield intense relations not resembling those that are institutionalized. It seems to me that a way of life can yield a culture and an ethics. To be 'gay,' I think, is not to identify with the psychological traits and the visible masks of the homosexual but to try to define and develop a way of life.[113]

What marks this gay ethos, or way of life, is its constant urge to reinvent: 'One could perhaps say there is a "gay style," or at least that there is an ongoing attempt to recreate a certain style of existence, a form of existence or art of living, which might be called "gay".'[114] '[W]e have to create a gay life', Foucault enjoins readers of *The Advocate*, 'To *become*.'[115] The aim is thus not to rest content with the achievement of a sense of self but to constantly 'form oneself, to surpass oneself'.[116] Indeed, as he says, '[t]he relationships we have to have with ourselves are not ones of identity, rather, they must be relationships of differentiation, of creation, of innovation', and so forth.[117]

As the above references to relations of differentiation and the surpassing of determinate identities make clear, Foucault's *ethos*, despite its emphasis on self-elaboration, is not concerned with a self-mastery or a self-possession which would simply confirm the subject in his or her sovereignty. This is the second misguided characterization of Foucault's ethical project to which we adverted in our earlier discussion. Whilst certain of the Stoic sources from which Foucault derives his notion of ethics did undoubtedly evince a concern for such self-mastery,[118] Foucault in fact envisages something completely different. For him, ethics is, in major part, a *techne* for desubjectification and a practice of challenging oneself in order to disrupt given forms of subjectivity. And despite the concerns of Dews and others that 'it is difficult to see how in contemporary society any such turn towards an aesthetics of existence could be anything other than a reinforcement of social tendencies towards atomization',[119] the Foucaultian ethical project is in fact conducted in a field of alterity. The references in Foucault's late work to the relationships of *differentiation* that the subject maintains with itself, and to the ultimate *deferral* of the subject's sense of self, recall this fact. We thus maintain here that the subject of Foucault's late ethics is neither the familiar subject of liberal humanism with certain enduring and determinate properties, but nor is it a subject which tries to secure its proper borders and master itself. Rather, the late Foucaultian subject is a subject never sure of itself, an uneasy and relational subject constantly posed in exteriority. As Foucault repeatedly stresses, the ethical subject he envisions is not one which resides in comfortable enclosure and satisfaction with its true sense of self but rather is turned outward to others in denial of any innate or fixed interiority. In affirming a subject always outside of itself Foucault is in fact aiming at the dissolution of fixed notions of subjectivity and advocating the embrace of relations of non-identity and differentiation. Hence the much derided (or welcomed) 'return of the subject' in the late Foucault constitutes not exactly a return but in large part a dispersal of traditional philosophical conceptions of subjectivity. Michael Hardt and Antonio Negri put it neatly in *Empire*, answering their own question about the intent of Foucault's late work:

> How is it possible that the author who worked so hard to convince us of the death of Man, the thinker who carried the banner of antihumanism throughout his career, would in the end champion these central tenets of the humanist tradition? We do not mean to suggest that Foucault contradicts himself or that he reversed his earlier position; he was always so insistent about the continuity of his discourse. Rather, Foucault asks in his final work a paradoxical and urgent question: What is humanism after the death of Man? Or rather, what is an antihumanist (or posthuman) humanism?[120]

Following Hardt and Negri's suggestion, we can perceive in Foucault's ethics an 'affirmation of being human beyond any known humanism',[121] an unconditional affirmation which 'does not stop, as liberalism does, at the individual as the "last instance" of freedom',[122] but rather puts the limits of that individual constantly in question. As Sergei Prozorov puts it:

> It is in this sense that Foucault's ontology may be said to postulate a 'human nature', with a caveat that the content of this 'nature' is entirely exhausted by the unnameable exteriority of the outside that exceeds every historically conditioned mode of subjectivity.[123]

So, *contra* those critics who read in Foucault a retreat or a return to a domain of self-enclosed subjectivity, the late work actually confirms for us that the Foucaultian subject cannot exist in replete self-sufficiency but in fact is formed in and through its responsive relation to others. It is in the space of that relation, in what Judith Butler (in engagement with Foucault) defines as a space of ontological insecurity,[124] that subjects broach their limits and discover 'relationships of differentiation, of creation, of innovation'[125] with themselves and invent 'a multiplicity of relationships' with others.[126] As Foucault remarks in an interview with Duccio Trombadori, from 1978:

[I]n the course of their history, men have never ceased to construct themselves, that is, to continually displace their subjectivity, to constitute themselves in an infinite, multiple series of different subjectivities that will never have an end and never bring us in the presence of something that would be 'man'. Men are perpetually engaged in a process that, in constituting objects, at the same time displaces man, deforms, transforms, and transfigures him as a subject.[127]

This process, a process in which 'man produces man', means that 'what ought to be produced is not man as nature supposedly designed him, or as his essence ordains him to be – we need to produce something that doesn't exist yet, without being able to know what it will be'.[128] It is precisely to the production of this ontological insecurity and the unsettling of who 'we' are as humans that the labour of Foucault's ethics is dedicated. Foucault's ethics represents an attempt to think ontology in a critical register, to live not according to a hermeneutic of ourselves that would seek to discover our true selves and then either liberate or renounce them, but to engage in an endless process of self-fashioning. Crucially, such an ethical project is not restricted to a question of personal or private behaviour (as the label 'ethics' might imply). As we have been arguing, it is important to grasp the specifically social dimension of Foucault's ethics. Foucault is providing a constituent model of *sociality*, of being-together, in which the transformation and displacement of 'one's' subjectivity takes place in a relational and contestatory field of affects, encounters and engagements with others.

Thus, the Foucaultian notion of ethical self-fashioning cannot be understood as a retreat from the stultifying normalization of social or institutional spaces to a properly private domain of protected difference. For Foucault, the tyranny of the social totality, of the spectre of a social closed onto and around itself, was always an explicit target of his critique. But it does not follow from this rejection of totality that Foucault retreats in the late work to a kind of individualism, opposing the normality of the social totality with the individualism of his ethics. Crucially, Foucault had always perceived the link between an increasing individualization and the reinforcement of a social totality, as his genealogical work on the modern specification of deviant and abnormal identities (the delinquent, the homosexual, the individual to be corrected, and so forth) amply attests. For Foucault, the primacy of the individual cannot resist the reification of the common because both entities partake in exactly the same totalizing (onto-)logic of closure:

> I think that the main characteristic of our political rationality is the fact that this integration of the individuals in a community or in a

totality results from a constant correlation between an increasing individualization and the reinforcement of this totality.[129]

And again:

> Very significantly, political criticism has reproached the state with being simultaneously a factor for individualization and a totalitarian principle. Just to look at nascent state rationality, just to see what its first policing project was, makes it clear that, right from the start, the state is both individualizing and totalitarian. Opposing the individual and his interests to it is just as hazardous as opposing it with the community and its requirements.[130]

We shall touch upon the notion of the community shortly, but as Jon Simons argues, developing explicitly the implicit political hazards of such a correlation between the individual and the social totality:

> Foucault holds that identity politics has its unbearably high costs. Identities are fashioned by political technologies of individuals which totalize as they individualize. On the basis of such identities we recognize ourselves as members of a social group or state. The same political logic according to which a gay man identifies himself politically as a member of the gay community induces citizens to lay down their lives in defence of their states. When identity is taken to be natural in relation to a larger social or political entity then, as Rajchman says, we are confronted by the identities of nationalism or racism. Not only are people tied to identities that are designed to be governable, but they are prepared to participate in mass sacrifice of themselves and others in wars to defend their identities.[131]

Patently, nothing could be further removed from Foucault's intentions. The late Foucaultian ethical project thus furnishes us with an example of a mode of being otherwise which does not simply aim to quarantine the individual from the networks of normalization and discipline but which, rather, tries to interrupt the political logic of closure that underpins the disciplinary formation of the social itself and in so doing to bring an openness to it. Foucault's ethics hence contemplates new and impermanent forms of sociality, constantly in the process of revision and contestation. His remarks on Deleuze and Guattari's *Anti-Oedipus* can stand as an effective description of his own theoretical position in this regard: 'What is needed is to "de-individualize" by means of multiplication and displacement, diverse combinations. The group must not be the organic bond uniting hierarchized individuals, but a constant generator of de-individualization.'[132] These diverse combinations and affective relationships can never be allowed to congeal into set dominations,[133] for 'society can exist only by means of the work it does on itself and on its institutions'.[134] In this we are 'always in the position of beginning again'.[135] It is this constituent attunement to alterity, to new ways of relating to others and of being-together, that constitutes the sociality of Foucault's ethical project.

And whereas with Ewald's project of 'social law' law emerges as the condition of closure of the social and of allowing the social to 'see itself as one',[136] the law of Foucault's ethics is suffused with multiplicity and alterity. The law of Foucault's ethics imports an irrepressible and illimitable sociality, discernible in his late engagements with rights. When Foucault invokes rights in his late discussions of ethical self-formation, he gives them a central and constituent role.[137] As we shall see, however, these rights do not correspond to a determinate subject identity but rather reflect the unfinished subject of Foucaultian ethics. For example, we see Foucault make an appeal to the 'liberty of expression' and the 'liberty to manifest' one's sexual choice, a liberty expressed 'on the level of legislation'.[138] And we see him propose a 'new relational *right*', which, he explains, 'is the right to gain recognition in an institutional sense for the relations of one individual to another individual'.[139] And, finally, we see him argue that '[h]uman rights regarding sexuality are important' and that 'we have – and can have – a right to be free'.[140] We read these invocations of rights not (as some have done) as a curious redeployment of liberal human rights discourse by the *maître-penseur* of anti-humanism[141] but rather as a notion of rights being always beyond themselves, being always beyond the existent. Just as Foucault's ethical subject is a subject outside itself, so too does his notion of rights concern a concept of rights not limited by any determinate content but one which must have a responsive regard to future emanations of the human. Hence we see Foucault, in a late interview on the technologies of the self, making a link between the critique of the limits of humanism and a thinking of human rights that sees it as constituently open to alterity and to the unforeseeable 'inventions' of futurity:

> Through these different practices – psychological, medical, penitential, educational – a certain idea or model of humanity was developed, and now this idea of man has become normative, self-evident, and is supposed to be universal. Humanism may not be universal but may be quite relative to a certain situation. What we call humanism has been used by Marxists, liberals, Nazis, Catholics. This does not

mean that we have to get rid of what we call human rights or freedom, but that we can't say that freedom or human rights has to be
limited at certain frontiers. For instance, if you asked eighty years
ago if feminine virtue was part of universal humanism, everyone
would have answered yes. What I am afraid of about humanism is
that it presents a certain form of our ethics as a universal model for
any kind of freedom. I think that there are more secrets, more
possible freedoms, and more inventions in our future than we can
imagine in humanism as it is dogmatically represented on every side
of the political rainbow: the Left, the Center, the Right.[142]

Foucault's understanding of rights as developed in the late work hence
relies upon a constituent instability and responsive regard to what is to
come. 'One must guard against reintroducing a hegemonic thought on the
pretext of presenting a human rights theory or policy', Foucault warns.[143]
Rights, if they are to be the carrier of future inventions and different
ways of being, must necessarily be 'unrestricted'.[144] It is this illimitability of rights that is central for Foucault, for this is the key to their
sustaining futurity. Were rights to be restricted to a determinate content, were they to ossify or reintroduce a hegemonic understanding of
what it means to be human or of what it means to be a part of a social
group, then the ability of rights to generate a continuate sociality would
be lost. As Foucault stresses, it is only through the work of altering
itself and differing from itself that society manages to continue in being.
This work both 'marks a relation of belonging and presents itself as a
task',[145] a task which is always ongoing and never fully achieved.

CONCLUSION: THE LAW OF SOCIALITY

The argument of this final chapter has sought to amplify the argument
advanced in the previous chapter. In Chapter 2, we contended that
Foucault's law was not in fact surpassed by, nor was it totally subordinated to, the dominant power forms of modernity that Foucault
sketches in his genealogical works of the mid-1970s: disciplinary power,
bio-power and governmentality. Rather, we argued that Foucault's law
demonstrated a capacity to be other to itself, to be responsive to the
irreducible movements of resistance which impinged upon or assailed its
determinate position. This more poststructuralist rendition of Foucault's
law saw law as that which could never be simply 'expelled' or rejected, but
rather demonstrated how law – in its incessant and unresolved movement
from determinacy to responsiveness – revealed a sustaining ability to

become other to itself. This potentiality, we argued, was the key to the perdurance of Foucault's law – whilst it could be subjected to the dictates of a seemingly predominant power (as Foucault's many discussions of the disciplinary invasion or occupation of law reveal), a total encapsulation of law was impossible. This self-resistant, responsive dimension of law, in which exteriority was itself formative of law, was evoked for us most suggestively in Foucault's engagement with the work of Maurice Blanchot which we discussed towards the end of the last chapter. There we encountered Foucault tracing the movement of a law which goes 'ever farther into the outside into which it is always receding',[146] the 'very movement by which', Blanchot reminds us, 'it formulates this exteriority as law'.[147]

In this chapter, we have sought to extend our re-interpretation of Foucault's law by arguing not simply that law remains in Foucault's modernity but rather that this conception of law is central to an experience of modernity. In so doing, we have tried in the foregoing discussion to relate Foucault's law to a thinking of sociality. Our central argument has been that law represents a key modality of our sociality, of our continuate being-with each other. Through its ability to combine iteratively a determinate securing of limits and a responsive regard to the disruption of those limits and their re-formation, law provides an opening to futurity. Law convokes a delimitable presence for a society but never imports a closure or a cohering of that society (rather being dedicated to its unworking, its constant unfolding, its sharing and spacing).[148] This is the law of the law, or law's sociality. In looking at these dual imperatives of law – a determination of the social and an opening of the social to alterity and to the inventions of the future – we addressed two different Foucaultian figures of law. First, we looked at Ewald's notion of 'social law' and tried to show how this approach, if taken to its limits, represented a closure of society onto itself and a denial of society's ability to be otherwise. Second, we turned to Foucault's own late writings on ethics and critical ontology in order to propose a counterpoint to the legal cohesion of Ewald's model. There we found a model of legality which was utterly responsive to the lability and futural contingency of the social, a law of alterity which was figured not simply in Foucault's discussions of ethics and critical ontology but, in a more directly legal vein, in his later discussions of rights as being illimitable and open to future inventions of the human. It is in its ultimate responsiveness to the changing contours of society that law finds its law of sociality.

As we signalled at the beginning of this chapter, our reading of the constituent sociality of Foucault's law is our development of his thought, and does not represent something which Foucault ever explicitly thematized in the way in which we have been doing in this chapter. Whilst this development of Foucault's thought is in line with his own critical enterprise, and whilst the components of this development are incipiently contained within Foucault's work, perhaps our engagement with Foucault here does constitute something of a provocation to Foucault in that it aims to 'stretch [his] ideas beyond their reach and intent'.[149] We want to conclude here with a reading which expresses this interpretive desire to take Foucault beyond Foucault (or to find within Foucault's work the means for thinking Foucault otherwise). In these closing pages, then, we offer a reading of Foucault's text, 'Truth and Juridical Forms', which seeks to press Foucault's thought further. This text is a collection of five lectures which Foucault delivered in Brazil in 1973 and in which Foucault conducts a sweeping genealogical survey of the function of law as a means of providing society's truth. In the first three lectures, Foucault offers some insights into the constituent sociality of law, along the very lines we have been developing in this chapter. In these reflections, law is revealed as a 'generative locus' for the production of a society's truth,[150] and of our very existence in and as society. Through its articulation of the relations between subjects, law constitutes the truth of the social bond. However, in the closing two lectures Foucault disappointingly shifts his emphasis from the centrality of law and juridical forms to the emergent disciplinary techniques of modernity (in line with the 'expulsion thesis' we criticized in Chapter 1). Our reading, then, aims to bring to bear upon the Foucault of the final lectures of 'Truth and Juridical Forms' the insights derived from our reading of Foucault in Chapter 2 and the present chapter. We want thus to develop Foucault's promising statements on law and on the constituent centrality of the juridical form to a thinking of society.

Foucault commences his discussion of the historical development of juridical forms with a discussion of Homer. In this discussion we can see how law is of central importance for determining the truth of the social bond:

> The first evidence we have of the search for truth in Greek judicial procedure dates back to the *Iliad*. It appears in the story of the dispute between Antilochus and Menelaus during the games organized to mark the death of Patroclus. Among these games there is a chariot race that is run, as usual, in an out-and-back circuit, going around a post that has to be passed as closely as possible. The games' organizers have placed a man there to make sure the rules of the race are followed; Homer, without naming him personally, says this man is a witness, *histor*, one who is there to see. The race

unfolds and the men in the lead at the turn are Antilochus and Menelaus. An infringement occurs and, when Antilochus arrives first, Menelaus lodges a protest and says to the judge, or to the jury who must award the prize, that Antilochus committed a foul. Protest, dispute – how is the truth to be established?[151]

The dispute between Antilochus and Menelaus is not resolved by resorting to the *histor*, to the one who is there to see, but rather by way of an oath – or, rather, by Antilochus' failure to swear an oath by Zeus. Foucault comments:

> This is a peculiar way to produce truth, to establish juridical truth – not through the testimony of a witness but through a sort of testing game, a challenge hurled by one adversary at another. If by chance he had accepted the risk, if he had actually sworn, the responsibility for what would happen, the final uncovering of the truth would immediately devolve upon the gods. And it would be Zeus who, by punishing the one who uttered the false oath if that were the case, would have manifested the truth with his thunderbolt.
>
> Here we have the old and very archaic practice of the test of truth, where the latter is established judicially not by an investigation, a witness, an inquiry, or an inquisition but, rather, by a testing game.[152]

Foucault next proceeds to a discussion of Sophocles' *Oedipus Rex*, which he reads as a 'kind of compendium of the history of Greek law'.[153] Sophocles' play stages the transition from a Homeric 'test of truth' (as instanced in the chariot-racing dispute between Antilochus and Menelaus) to a new juridical regime for the enunciation of truth in ancient Greek society: the *inquiry*. As Foucault remarks, the 'remnants of the old tradition reappear at times over the length of the entire play', such as in the scene where Creon proposes to swear an oath in the presence of Jocasta that he did not distort the prophecy of the Delphic oracle.[154] However, despite such remnants of the earlier juridical form, the play ultimately marks 'a way of shifting the enunciation of the truth from a prophetic and prescriptive type of discourse to a retrospective one that is no longer characterized by prophecy but, rather, by evidence'.[155] According to Foucault, we can see this definitive transition in juridical forms accomplished in the undoing of Oedipus. The truth of the Oedipal crime (Oedipus' killing of King Laius) is established not by way of test or ordeal but rather by way of the *histor* and his testimonial knowledge: 'The most humble slave of Polybus [Oedipus' adoptive father, the King of Corinth] and, decisively, the most hidden herdsman of the forest of

Cithaera pronounce the final truth and provide the final piece of evidence.'[156] As Foucault states:

> At the humblest level there is again a gaze – for, if the two slaves can testify, it's because they have seen. The first saw Jocasta place a child in his hands to be taken into the forest and abandoned; the second saw his fellow slave hand this child over to him and recalls having carried the child to Polybus' palace. It's still a matter of the gaze – no longer the great eternal, illuminating, dazzling, flashing gaze of the god and his prophet, but that of those persons who saw and remember having seen with their own human eyes. It is the gaze of the witness. It is the gaze that Homer made no reference to when he spoke of the conflict and formal dispute between Antilochus and Menelaus.[157]

Thus, with Sophocles' *Oedipus Rex* Greek society moves beyond a Homeric juridical form based upon the contest and the ordeal to one based upon evidence supplied by a witness:

> That great conquest of Greek democracy, that right to bear witness, to oppose truth to power, was established in a long process born and instituted in a definitive way in Athens throughout the fifth century. That right to set a powerless truth against a truthless power gave rise to a series of major cultural forms that were characteristic of Greek society.[158]

As Foucault says in the above quotation, these juridical practices are themselves 'characteristic', indeed constitutive, of forms of Greek society. Law does not simply provide a mechanism for asserting the truth of a dispute or a controversy, but, more fundamentally, in its articulation of the changing relationships between subjects of law it represents the truth of the social bond itself. Tracing his genealogy of the juridical practices of truth-formation forward into early European societies in the third lecture, Foucault finds that the Greek form of the inquiry 'was lost ... [only to be] taken up again, in other forms, several centuries later, in the Middle Ages'.[159] In the interim, the old Germanic law actually rehearsed some of the same practices as the archaic Greek (Homeric) contest:

> The system that regulated conflicts and disputes in the Germanic societies of that era was therefore entirely governed by struggle and compromise, involving a test of strength that could end with an economic settlement. It depended on a procedure that did not allow for the intervention of a third individual who would stand between

the two others as a neutral party seeking the truth, trying to determine which of the two had told the truth. A procedure of inquiry, a search for the truth, never intervened in this type of system. This was how the old Germanic law was constituted, before the invasion of the Roman Empire.[160]

In such a system law functioned as the guarantee of a procedure of war, and not as a mechanism for securing the truth. Foucault does not 'linger over the long series of vicissitudes that brought this Germanic law into rivalry, competition, and at times collusion with Roman law',[161] but simply indicates how the Germanic system of the contest dominated the form of feudal law in the early Middle Ages. In the late Middle Ages, however, Foucault shows how with the rise of monarchical administrations and the emergence of centralized systems of sovereignty, 'state power appropriated the entire judicial procedure, the entire mechanism of interindividual settlement of disputes'[162] which had characterized the old Germanic-feudal system. As a consequence of this development:

> Thereafter individuals would no longer have the right to resolve their own disputes, whether regularly or irregularly; they would have to submit to a power external to them, imposing itself as a judicial political power.[163]

From this 'appropriation of the penal justice system by the state in the Middle Ages',[164] Foucault goes on to track the eventual emergence of the disciplinary society – a topic which he discusses in the fourth and fifth lectures of the series, presaging the publication of *Discipline and Punish* two years later. In these last two lectures, as we have indicated, Foucault places much less emphasis on the constituent centrality of law to the formation of the social and focuses instead to a greater degree upon modalities of discipline and social control which emerged 'next to and outside that state-controlled judicial system'.[165]

What we find, then, in Foucault's 'Truth and Juridical Forms' is the beginnings of the perspective we have been developing in this chapter. The abiding thematic of Foucault's discussion of law in the first three lectures of 'Truth and Juridical Forms' is the constituent centrality of law to the formation of the social bond. We thus see law emerge as a 'starting point'[166] for forms of knowledge and social organization, and as a 'mold' or 'model on the basis of which a series of other knowledges – philosophical, rhetorical, and empirical – were able to develop and characterize Greek [and later] thought'.[167] Indeed, as Foucault puts it at the very beginning of the series of lectures: 'There you have a general view of the theme I intend to develop: juridical forms and their evolution in the field of penal law as the generative locus for a given number of forms of truth.'[168] Yet in other places Foucault hesitates to accord law such a significant role, arguing that it is merely 'one of the forms' by which society organizes itself,[169] and, as we indicated above, in the last two lectures of the series Foucault does tend to focus much more upon the emergent disciplinary logics of modern society.

Our reading of Foucault in this book, however, has in fact shown how (through a re-reading of Foucault's own writings) law cannot be definitively subdued, 'expelled' or marginalized in modernity. Foucault's law, in the way in which we have developed it throughout this book, reveals its suscitating ability to become other to itself. Whilst law in Foucault's account is indeed made subordinate to disciplinary formations in a 'perpetual reference to something other than itself', such an 'unceasing re-inscription in non-juridical systems' does not,[170] *pace* those proponents of the 'expulsion thesis', betoken the end or the subsumption of law in modernity. Rather, if on occasion the 'counter-law [disciplinary power] becomes the effective and institutionalized content of the juridical forms',[171] then this movement and investment attest to law's necessary responsiveness, to its orientation towards an outside. Such disciplinary invasions of law evidence law's lack of enduring content, its ultimate vacuity. Crucially, as we showed towards the end of Chapter 2, this vacuity of Foucault's law means that it can never be fully appropriated or rendered in any set or determinate terms by powers outside it. And, connecting that thought in the present setting to the question of social organization in modernity, we have tried to show how this sustaining, responsive quality of Foucault's law makes it a pre-eminent, 'generative locus' for the production of a society's truth.[172] Foucault's law, through its futural opening to and for society, through its responsiveness, is the truth of the social bond. As the genealogical trend of Foucault's discussion of law in 'Truth and Juridical Forms' makes abundantly clear, law does not and cannot provide a singular and enduring truth for society (indeed, as he says, law and its truth are 'constantly modified through the course of history').[173] Rather, law as the truth of the social bond, of our being-with each other, must be a mobile and contingent truth. As we have been arguing throughout this chapter and the previous one, such an ever-revisable truth would be the only basis for our continuate existence as society. Far from being expelled, then, Foucault's law emerges in our account as a constituent means of our securing this being-together, of our living this tenuous truth of society. Such an account reads the responsiveness and necessary vacuity of Foucault's law not as a sign of its demise but, rather, as the promise of its future.

Notes

1 Helene Cixous, speaking about Foucault, quoted in Timothy O'Leary, *Foucault: The Art of Ethics* (London: Continuum, 2002), p. 171.

2 As per Giorgio Agamben, *Homo Sacer: Sovereign Power and Bare Life*, trans. Daniel Heller-Roazen (Stanford, CA: Stanford University Press, 1998), p. 9.

3 For an 'unfaithful' interpretation of Foucault which is nevertheless faithful to a certain Foucaultian *ethos*, see Sergei Prozorov, *Foucault, Freedom and Sovereignty* (Aldershot: Ashgate, 2007), pp. 14–21.

4 Michel Foucault, 'Prison Talk', in *Power/Knowledge: Selected Interviews and Other Writings 1972–1977*, trans. Colin Gordon *et al.*, ed. Colin Gordon (Brighton: Harvester Press, 1980), pp. 37–54 (pp. 53–54). This approach to Foucault's thought is consonant with Foucault's other well known observations on the use of theory as a 'toolkit' or a 'tool-box'. For example, see 'Intellectuals and Power: A Conversation between Michel Foucault and Gilles Deleuze', in *Language, Counter-Memory, Practice: Selected Essays and Interviews*, trans. Donald F. Bouchard and Sherry Simon, ed. Donald F. Bouchard (Ithaca, NY: Cornell University Press, 1977), pp. 205–17 (p. 208); Michel Foucault, 'Powers and Strategies', in *Power/Knowledge*, pp. 134–45 (p. 145); Michel Foucault, 'Questions on Geography', in *Power/Knowledge*, pp. 62–77 (p. 65); Michel Foucault, 'Des supplices aux cellules', *Le Monde*, 21 February 1975, quoted in Didier Eribon, *Michel Foucault*, trans. Betsy Wing (Cambridge, MA: Harvard University Press, 1991), p. 237. In another interview from 1975, with Jean-Louis Ezine, Foucault stresses: 'I certainly do not see what I do as a body of work [*oeuvre*], and I am shocked to see anyone can call me a writer ... I sell tools' (Michel Foucault, 'Sur la sellette', *Les Nouvelles littéraires*, 17 March 1975, quoted in David Macey, *The Lives of Michel Foucault* (New York: Vintage, 1993), p. xxi).

5 Jacques Derrida makes a crucial distinction in his work between two notions of the future. The first notion is the idea of the future as a programmable and foreseeable horizon, as that which can be actualized and somehow brought to presence. This is the idea of the 'future present'. The other, more radical idea of the future is thematized by Derrida under the name of the *à-venir*, the 'to come'. This is the idea of the future as that which can never be accounted for in advance, as 'something that is structurally and necessarily to come, always still outstanding, never present', a concept which thus 'deprives the present of its prestige and exposes it to something *tout autre*, "wholly other," beyond what is foreseeable from the present, beyond the horizon of the "same"' (John D. Caputo, 'Deconstruction in a Nutshell: The Very Idea (!)', in *Deconstruction in a Nutshell: A Conversation with Jacques Derrida*, ed. John D. Caputo (New York: Fordham University Press, 1997), pp. 31–48 (p. 42) (emphasis in original)). For a discussion of the difference between these two notions of the future – the 'future present' and the 'to come' – in relation to law and justice, see Jacques Derrida, 'Force of Law: The "Mystical Foundation of Authority"', trans. Mary Quaintance, in *Acts of Religion*, ed. Gil Anidjar (New York: Routledge, 2002), pp. 228–98 (p. 256). Our notion of law's futurity is intended to convey both these orientations towards a future. Law must necessarily attempt to plan and arrange for future events and to make some determinate provision for the future, to bring the future into the present and to

actualize it in the existent. This is the idea of law incorporatively engaging with a future, bringing a future to its determinate position. But equally law becomes undone by a future, by what comes and remains to come, by the 'wholly other' which utterly vacates that determinate position.

6 Michel Foucault, *The Archaeology of Knowledge*, trans. A. M. Sheridan Smith (London: Routledge, 1972), p. 131.
7 Michel Foucault, 'A Preface to Transgression', in *Language, Counter-Memory, Practice*, pp. 29–52.
8 The Nietzschean reference is to Friedrich Nietzsche, *The Gay Science*, trans. Josefine Nauckhoff, ed. Bernard Williams (Cambridge: Cambridge University Press, 2001), pp. 119–20, § 125.
9 Foucault, 'A Preface to Transgression', p. 30.
10 *Ibid.*, p. 50.
11 *Ibid.*, p. 32.
12 *Ibid.*, p. 37.
13 *Ibid.*, p. 34.
14 *Ibid.*, p. 32.
15 For what have now become definitive tropes of the experience of modernity, see William Butler Yeats, 'The Second Coming', in *Selected Poems*, ed. Timothy Webb (Harmondsworth: Penguin, 2000), p. 124, and Karl Marx and Friedrich Engels, *The Communist Manifesto* (Harmondsworth: Penguin, 1967), p. 83.
16 Douglas Litowitz, 'Foucault on Law: Modernity as Negative Utopia' (1995) 21 *Queen's Law Journal* 1.
17 Or, in Jon Simons's phrase, that Foucault has in places become 'a prophet of entrapment who induces despair by indicating that there is no way out of our subjection' (Jon Simons, *Foucault and the Political* (London: Routledge, 1995), p. 3).
18 Some of these sources were discussed in Chapter 1. The sources we rely upon here in reconstructing Ewald's account of the social logic of modern law are: François Ewald, 'A Concept of Social Law', trans. Iain Fraser, in *Dilemmas of Law in the Welfare State*, ed. Gunther Teubner (New York and Berlin: Walter de Gruyter, 1988), pp. 40–75; François Ewald, 'The Law of Law', trans. Iain Fraser, in *Autopoietic Law: A New Approach to Law and Society*, ed. Gunther Teubner (New York and Berlin: Walter de Gruyter, 1988), pp 36–50; François Ewald, 'Justice, Equality, Judgement: On "Social Justice"', trans. Iain Fraser, in *Juridification of Social Spheres: A Comparative Analysis in the Areas of Labor, Corporate, Antitrust and Social Welfare Law*, ed. Gunther Teubner (New York and Berlin: Walter de Gruyter, 1987), pp. 91–110; François Ewald, 'Foucault and the Contemporary Scene', trans. Richard A. Lynch (1999) 25 *Philosophy & Social Criticism* 81.
19 Ewald, 'The Law of Law', p. 36.
20 *Ibid.*, p. 38 (emphasis in original).
21 *Ibid.*, p. 37.
22 *Ibid.*, p. 37.
23 *Ibid.*, p. 40.
24 *Ibid.*, p. 41.
25 *Ibid.*, p. 45.
26 *Ibid.*, p. 38.
27 *Ibid.*, p. 44.
28 Ewald, 'Justice, Equality, Judgement', p. 106.

29 Ewald, 'A Concept of Social Law', p. 45.
30 Michel Foucault, 'Society Must Be Defended': Lectures at the Collège de France, 1975–76, trans. David Macey (London: Allen Lane, 2003), p. 18.
31 Ewald, 'A Concept of Social Law', p. 46.
32 Ibid., p. 46.
33 Ibid., p. 46.
34 Ibid., p. 48.
35 Ibid., p. 58.
36 Ibid., pp. 53, 50.
37 Ibid., pp. 56–57.
38 Ibid., p. 68 (emphasis in original). See also our discussion of Ewald and the jurisprudence of the norm in Chapter 1, in the section entitled 'The "juridical" and the "legal"'. In that context we focused upon the argument made by Ewald (in his influential text, 'Norms, Discipline, and the Law') that the terms 'law' and 'juridical' were not synonymous in Foucault's work and that whilst law had not been expelled in Foucault's work (contra the argument of Alan Hunt and Gary Wickham, Foucault and Law: Towards a Sociology of Law as Governance (London: Pluto Press, 1994), discussed in the preceding chapters), it had fundamentally changed its character in modernity by becoming aligned with the norm (in the sense for which Foucault is renowned – on this, see Chapter 1, note 43). See François Ewald, 'Norms, Discipline, and the Law', trans. Marjorie Beale, in Law and the Order of Culture, ed. Robert Post (Berkeley, CA: University of California Press, 1991), pp. 138–61. Our critique of this position in Chapter 1 was that it tended to elide the difference between law and norm which was central for Foucault. Our critique of Ewald's position in the present context is somewhat different in that here we are arguing against Ewald's acceptance of the norm as a socially just measure of cohesion.
39 Ewald, 'Justice, Equality, Judgement', p. 107.
40 Ewald, 'A Concept of Social Law', p. 62. Ewald is here expressly discussing the notion of balancing, but he goes on in the same piece to explain on p. 68 how '[a] judgment of balance, in the social law sense, is a normative [in the sense used by Foucault] judgment' (emphasis in original).
41 Ibid., p. 70.
42 Ewald, 'Justice, Equality, Judgement', p. 107.
43 Ewald, 'A Concept of Social Law', p. 70.
44 Ewald, 'Justice, Equality, Judgement', p. 107.
45 Ibid., p. 108.
46 Ibid., p. 108.
47 Ibid., p. 108 (emphasis in original).
48 Ewald does, as we have mentioned above, characterize the social as a space of dispersion and dislocation. Furthermore, he does characterize the operation of the norm as one of 'perpetual claiming' as opposed to 'final consent' (ibid., p. 107). The norm, he says in the same text, is a 'yardstick that society equips itself with in order to follow its own transformations, and that transforms itself, and this is the point, along with the transformations that it describes' (ibid., p. 107). Elsewhere, Ewald stresses that the judgment of balance (a concept he later links with the norm) 'must be a flexible judgment; it must always be able to adapt to history, to development, to social change' (Ewald, 'A Concept of Social Law', p. 66). So, when we argue that Ewald's articulation of the law of the law moves in the direction of the

cohesion of society, we do not thereby mean to imply some kind of legal stasis (such would, following our arguments in the previous chapter, be an impossibility). Rather, we simply mean that the orientation of Ewald's law is to contain the fecundity of the social. The trend of Ewald's argument is towards this pacification, whereas what we go on to articulate now is a sociality of law that is dedicated to unworking instantiations of the social.

49 Michel Foucault, 'What is Enlightenment?', in *Essential Works of Foucault 1954–1984, Vol. 1: Ethics, Subjectivity and Truth*, trans. Robert Hurley *et al.*, ed. Paul Rabinow (Harmondsworth: Allen Lane/Penguin, 1997), pp. 303–19 (p. 309).

50 It is surprising in both a specific and a general sense. That Kant is singled out for praise in this later work contradicts Foucault's earlier trenchant criticism of the philosopher in *The Order of Things* as having reduced modern philosophy to anthropology, in the sense of making subsequent philosophical reflection turn upon the essence and nature of 'man'. See Michel Foucault, *The Order of Things: An Archaeology of the Human Sciences*, trans. Alan Sheridan (New York: Vintage Books, 1994), pp. 303–43. In a more general sense, it may be surprising – indeed it definitely has proved so for several readers of the text – to see Foucault attempt to reposition himself in an Enlightenment narrative of critique towards which he was supposedly inimical. For a neat summary of this scholarly surprise and the grounds for it, see Amy Allen, 'Foucault and Enlightenment: A Critical Reappraisal' (2003) 10 *Constellations* 180.

51 See Immanuel Kant, 'An Answer to the Question: "What is Enlightenment?"', in *Political Writings*, trans. H. B. Nisbet, ed. H. S. Reiss (Cambridge: Cambridge University Press, 1970), pp. 54–60.

52 Foucault, 'What is Enlightenment?', p. 309.

53 *Ibid.*, p. 311.

54 *Ibid.*, p. 313.

55 *Ibid.*, p. 313.

56 *Ibid.*, p. 314.

57 *Ibid.*, p. 316.

58 *Ibid.*, p. 315 (emphasis in original).

59 *Ibid.*, p. 319.

60 *Ibid.*, p. 319.

61 Ewald, 'Foucault and the Contemporary Scene', p. 87.

62 Michel Foucault, *Discipline and Punish: The Birth of the Prison*, trans. Alan Sheridan (Harmondsworth: Penguin, 1991), p. 106.

63 *Ibid.*, p. 66.

64 Claude Lefort, *The Political Forms of Modern Society: Bureaucracy, Democracy, Totalitarianism*, ed. John B. Thompson (Cambridge: Polity Press, 1986), p. 207.

65 *Ibid.*, p. 201.

66 Paul Rabinow, 'Introduction: The History of Systems of Thought', in *Essential Works of Foucault, Vol. 1: Ethics*, pp. xi–xlii (p. xxxix).

67 *Le Robert*, quoted in *ibid.*, p. xxxix.

68 François Delaporte, quoted in *ibid.*, p. xl.

69 For a discussion of the planned, and subsequently revised, publication timetable of the *History of Sexuality* project, see Eribon, *Michel Foucault*, pp. 317–21.

70 Michel Foucault, 'Technologies of the Self', in *Essential Works of Foucault, Vol. 1: Ethics*, pp. 223–51 (p. 225).

71 For an excellent and lucid overview of some of these themes in both Foucault's work and the subsequent literature on governmentality, see David Garland, '"Governmentality" and the Problem of Crime: Foucault, Criminology, Sociology' (1997) 1 *Theoretical Criminology* 173.

72 Barry Smart, 'On the Subjects of Sexuality, Ethics, and Politics in the Work of Foucault' (1991) 18 *boundary 2* 201, 204. See also our discussion in Chapter 1, note 35.

73 Michel Foucault, 'On the Genealogy of Ethics: An Overview of Work in Progress', in Hubert L. Dreyfus and Paul Rabinow, *Michel Foucault: Beyond Structuralism and Hermeneutics*, 2nd edn (Chicago: University of Chicago Press, 1983), pp. 229–52 (pp. 237–38) (emphasis in original).

74 What follows is taken from *ibid.*, pp. 238–43.

75 *Ibid.*, p. 238.

76 *Ibid.*, p. 239.

77 *Ibid.*, p. 239.

78 For example, see Emmanuel Levinas, 'Ethics as First Philosophy', trans. Seán Hand and Michael Temple, in *The Levinas Reader*, ed. Seán Hand (Oxford: Basil Blackwell, 1989), pp. 75–87; Emmanuel Levinas, 'Transcendence and Height', trans. Simon Critchley, in *Emmanuel Levinas: Basic Philosophical Writings*, ed. Adriaan T. Peperzak, Simon Critchley, and Robert Bernasconi (Bloomington and Indianapolis: Indiana University Press, 1996), pp. 11–30. Whereas for Levinas the relation to the Other ontologically precedes the self, the ethical understanding of the ancient Greeks placed an emphasis upon the ontological primacy of the self. As Foucault explains, '[t]he care of the self is ethically prior in that the relationship with oneself is ontologically prior' (see Michel Foucault, 'The Ethics of the Concern of the Self as a Practice of Freedom', in *Essential Works of Foucault, Vol. 1: Ethics*, pp. 281–301 (p. 287)). Statements such as these from Foucault are frequently adduced to demonstrate that his ethical understanding is not in fact concerned with questions of responsiveness and alterity but rather with self-possession and self-mastery. As our reading below maintains, this is to miss the point that Foucault's own re-deployment of ancient Greek ethics is intended, at least in part, as an exercise in self-dissolution and de-subjectification.

79 This is the main argument of Eric Paras, *Foucault 2.0: Beyond Power and Knowledge* (New York: Other Press, 2006).

80 Peter Dews, *Logics of Disintegration: Post-structuralist Thought and the Claims of Critical Theory* (London: Verso, 1987), p. 156; Peter Dews, 'The Return of the Subject in Late Foucault' (1989) 51 *Radical Philosophy* 37, 38. Or, in the pithier terms of J. G. Merquior, from this perspective Foucault's late work on the self-constitutive possibilities of subjects introduces a shift from a conception of subjectivity as a 'dependent variable (historical product of power)' to an 'independent variable' (J. G. Merquior, *Foucault* (London: Fontana, 1985), p. 138).

81 Foucault, 'The Ethics of the Concern of the Self as a Practice of Freedom', p. 293.

82 *Ibid.*, p. 291.

83 Judith Butler, 'What is Critique? An Essay on Foucault's Virtue', in *The Judith Butler Reader*, ed. Sara Salih with Judith Butler (Oxford: Blackwell, 2004), pp. 304–22 (p. 321).

84 Foucault, 'The Ethics of the Concern of the Self as a Practice of Freedom', p. 290.

85 Michel Foucault, *The Will to Knowledge: The History of Sexuality, Vol. 1*, trans. Robert Hurley (Harmondsworth: Penguin, 1979), pp. 17–49.

86 Foucault, 'On the Genealogy of Ethics', p. 245.

87 Timothy O'Leary's interpretation of the political goal of Foucault's late ethical project is that it is a reaction to this Christian hermeneutic, and it is an interpretation with which we are in broad agreement here. See O'Leary, *Foucault: The Art of Ethics*, p. 38. The reader should also bear in mind Foucault's own professed reasons for the return to classical Greek sources on sexuality. See, for example, Michel Foucault, 'Preface to *The History of Sexuality*, Volume Two', in *Essential Works of Foucault, Vol. 1: Ethics*, pp. 199–205; Michel Foucault, *The Use of Pleasure: The History of Sexuality, Vol. 2*, trans. Robert Hurley (Harmondsworth: Penguin, 1992), pp. 3–13.

88 See Simons, *Foucault and the Political*, pp. 71–72; Foucault, 'On the Genealogy of Ethics', p. 230.

89 Michel Foucault, 'The Battle for Chastity', in *Essential Works of Foucault, Vol. 1: Ethics*, pp. 185–97 (p. 195). Whilst verbal confession comes to be the primary vehicle for this hermeneutic, historically it is not the only practice. See Foucault's discussion in 'Technologies of the Self', on pp. 242–49, of the practices of *exomologēsis* and *exagoreusis* in the early Christian church. Foucault does not give precise definitions of the Greek terms, but the former is a practice whereby the penitent publicly manifests his status as a sinner through certain ritual, symbolic and theatrical gestures, whereas the latter was a process of self-examination developed in monastic contexts whereby the monk manifested his perpetual obedience to his spiritual director.

90 Michel Foucault, 'Sexuality and Solitude', in *Essential Works of Foucault, Vol. 1: Ethics*, pp. 175–84 (p. 178).

91 *Ibid.*, p. 178.

92 *Ibid.*, p. 182.

93 Foucault, 'Technologies of the Self', p. 245.

94 *Ibid.*, p. 249.

95 Foucault, *Discipline and Punish*, p. 294.

96 Michel Foucault, '"*Omnes et Singulatim*": Toward a Critique of Political Reason', in *Essential Works of Foucault 1954–1984, Vol. 3: Power*, trans. Robert Hurley *et al.*, ed. James D. Faubion (New York: New Press, 2000), pp. 298–325 (p. 312).

97 'If I tell the truth about myself, as I am now doing, it is in part that I am constituted as a subject across a number of power relations which are exerted over me and which I exert over others. I say this in order to situate what for me is the question of power' (Michel Foucault, 'Critical Theory/Intellectual History', in *Politics, Philosophy, Culture: Interviews and Other Writings, 1977–1984*, trans. Alan Sheridan *et al.*, ed. Lawrence D. Kritzman (London: Routledge, 1988), pp. 17–46 (p. 39)).

98 Michel Foucault, 'Friendship as a Way of Life', in *Essential Works of Foucault, Vol. 1: Ethics*, pp. 135–40 (p. 137).

99 Michel Foucault, 'What is Critique?', trans. Kevin Paul Geiman, in *What is Enlightenment? Eighteenth-Century Answers and Twentieth-Century Questions*, ed. James Schmidt (Berkeley and Los Angeles: University of California Press, 1996), pp. 382–98 (p. 386).

100 Michel Foucault, 'The Subject and Power', in *Essential Works of Foucault, Vol. 3: Power*, pp. 326–48 (p. 336).
101 Foucault, 'On the Genealogy of Ethics', p. 235 (emphasis in original).
102 *Ibid.*, p. 230.
103 *Ibid.*, p. 245 (emphasis in original).
104 Michel Foucault, 'An Aesthetics of Existence', in *Politics, Philosophy, Culture*, pp. 47–53 (p. 49).
105 *Ibid.*, p. 49.
106 Foucault, 'On the Genealogy of Ethics', p. 237.
107 Foucault, 'Friendship as a Way of Life', p. 137.
108 Foucault, 'The Ethics of the Concern of the Self as a Practice of Freedom', p. 282.
109 Michel Foucault, 'The Minimalist Self', in *Politics, Philosophy, Culture*, pp. 3–16 (p. 14).
110 For Foucault, techniques as diverse as Christian modalities of confession and psychoanalytic therapy were 'hermeneutic' in the sense that they attempted to interpret the truth of a subject, an idea which he was seeking to contest. See Michel Foucault, 'About the Beginning of the Hermeneutics of the Self: Two Lectures at Dartmouth' (1993) 21 *Political Theory* 198.
111 It is important to stress that for Foucault, as for Nietzsche, classical studies could have no meaning if they were not *untimely* – in that sense, as Nietzsche elegantly puts it at the beginning of 'On the Uses and Disadvantages of History for Life', of 'acting counter to our time and thereby acting on our time and, let us hope, for the benefit of a time to come' (Friedrich Nietzsche, 'On the Uses and Disadvantages of History for Life', trans. R. J. Hollingdale, in *Untimely Meditations*, ed. Daniel Breazeale (Cambridge: Cambridge University Press, 1997), pp. 59–123 (p. 60)). The return to Greece is hence not simply a learned divagation but rather a genealogy with political motivations in the present. As we have been arguing here, the political motivation is to derive a model of resistant ethical subjectivity from the ancient Greek texts which can be put to use to contest contemporary hermeneutics of the self. Some of the best examples of how Foucault mobilizes these concepts in a contemporary setting are to be found in his writings on gay subjectivity. However, Foucault's reliance on ancient Greek ethics does *not* mean that Foucault perceives the past as an unqualified solution to the political questions of the present. The Greeks provide a generative impetus but not a ready-made solution. On this, see Foucault, 'On the Genealogy of Ethics', pp. 231–32, 234.
112 Foucault, 'Friendship as a Way of Life', pp. 135–36.
113 *Ibid.*, p. 138.
114 Michel Foucault, 'Sexual Choice, Sexual Act', in *Essential Works of Foucault, Vol. 1: Ethics*, pp. 141–56 (p. 146).
115 Michel Foucault, 'Sex, Power, and the Politics of Identity', in *Essential Works of Foucault, Vol. 1: Ethics*, pp. 163–73 (p. 163) (emphasis in original).
116 Foucault, 'The Ethics of the Concern of the Self as a Practice of Freedom', p. 285.
117 Foucault, 'Sex, Power, and the Politics of Identity', p. 166.
118 Michel Foucault, *Fearless Speech*, ed. Joseph Pearson (Los Angeles: Semiotext(e), 2001), p. 164. Cf. O'Leary, *Foucault: The Art of Ethics*, pp. 66–67.
119 Dews, 'The Return of the Subject in Late Foucault', p. 40. Cf. Jeffrey T. Nealon, *Foucault Beyond Foucault: Power and Its Intensifications since 1984* (Stanford, CA: Stanford University Press, 2008), pp. 11–12.

120 Michael Hardt and Antonio Negri, *Empire* (Cambridge, MA: Harvard University Press, 2000), p. 91. As Derrida helpfully reminds us, such a deconstructive project is anything but anti-humanist in nature: '[T]o be suspicious about the limits of man is not to be anti-humanist, on the contrary, it's a way of respecting what remains "to come", under the name and the face of what we call "man". You have to be more and more human, and it's not obvious what it means. We are not human enough, we are never human enough, so from that point of view unconditional hospitality is not restricted by what one knows under the name of man or what is proper to man. We have to be hospitable to what is coming, and to a new figure, a new shape of what one calls humanity' (Jacques Derrida, 'A Discussion with Jacques Derrida' (2001) 5 *Theory & Event* paras [1]–[49], para. [44]).
121 Sergei Prozorov, *Foucault, Freedom and Sovereignty* (Aldershot: Ashgate, 2007), p. 14.
122 *Ibid.*, p. 13.
123 *Ibid.*, p. 40.
124 Butler, 'What is Critique? An Essay on Foucault's Virtue', p. 321.
125 Foucault, 'Sex, Power, and the Politics of Identity', p. 166.
126 Foucault, 'Friendship as a Way of Life', p. 135.
127 Michel Foucault, 'Interview with Michel Foucault', in *Essential Works of Foucault, Vol. 3: Power*, pp. 239–97 (p. 276).
128 *Ibid.*, p. 275.
129 Michel Foucault, 'The Political Technology of Individuals', in *Essential Works of Foucault, Vol. 3: Power*, pp. 401–17 (p. 417).
130 Foucault, '"Omnes et Singulatim"', p. 325.
131 Simons, *Foucault and the Political*, p. 98. The reference is to John Rajchman, *Truth and Eros: Foucault, Lacan, and the Question of Ethics* (New York: Routledge, 1991), p. 103.
132 Michel Foucault, 'Preface to *Anti-Oedipus*', in *Essential Works of Foucault, Vol. 3: Power*, pp. 106–10 (p. 109).
133 See Foucault, 'The Subject and Power', pp. 340–48; Paul Patton, 'Foucault's Subject of Power', in *The Later Foucault: Politics and Philosophy*, ed. Jeremy Moss (London: Sage, 1998), pp. 64–77 (pp. 67–69).
134 Michel Foucault, 'Vous êtes dangereux', *Libération*, 10 June 1983, quoted in Eribon, *Michel Foucault*, p. 269.
135 Foucault, 'What is Enlightenment?', p. 317.
136 Ewald, 'Justice, Equality, Judgement', p. 108.
137 Note however his assessment that the practice of ancient Greek ethics took place outside the realms of the juridical (conceived as either a moral code or a system of obligations). On the separation of the classical *ethos* from the code of morality, see Foucault, *The History of Sexuality, Vol. 2*, pp. 32, 62, 91–93; Michel Foucault, *The Care of the Self: The History of Sexuality, Vol. 3*, trans. Robert Hurley (Harmondsworth: Penguin, 1990), pp. 40–41. See also Foucault, 'On the Genealogy of Ethics', pp. 231, 233, 235.
138 Foucault, 'Sexual Choice, Sexual Act', p. 143.
139 Michel Foucault, 'The Social Triumph of the Sexual Will', in *Essential Works of Foucault, Vol. 1: Ethics*, pp. 157–62 (pp. 160, 162). In the first quotation the emphasis is in the original.
140 Foucault, 'Sex, Power, and the Politics of Identity', pp. 164, 166.
141 For example, Paras, *Foucault 2.0*, p. 12.

142 Michel Foucault, quoted in Rux Martin, 'Truth, Power, Self: An Interview with Michel Foucault', in *Technologies of the Self: A Seminar with Michel Foucault*, ed. Luther H. Martin, Huck Gutman and Patrick H. Hutton (Amherst: University of Massachusetts Press, 1988), pp. 9–15 (p. 15).

143 Michel Foucault, 'The Moral and Social Experience of the Poles Can No Longer be Obliterated', in *Essential Works of Foucault, Vol. 3: Power*, pp. 465–73 (p. 472).

144 Michel Foucault, 'Useless to Revolt?', in *Essential Works of Foucault, Vol. 3: Power*, pp. 449–53 (p. 453).

145 Foucault, 'What is Enlightenment?', p. 309.

146 Michel Foucault, 'Maurice Blanchot: The Thought from Outside', trans. Brian Massumi, in *Foucault/Blanchot* (New York: Zone Books, 1987), pp. 9–58 (p. 34).

147 Maurice Blanchot, *The Infinite Conversation*, trans. Susan Hanson (Minneapolis and London: University of Minnesota Press, 1993), p. 434.

148 Such a formulation of sociality is indebted to Jean-Luc Nancy's articulation of community in *The Inoperative Community*, trans. Peter Connor *et al.* (Minneapolis: University of Minnesota Press, 1991) – see especially pp. xxxvi–xli, 1–42. And on law's relation to such, see Jean-Luc Nancy, *Being Singular Plural*, trans. Robert D. Richardson and Anne E. O'Byrne (Stanford, CA: Stanford University Press, 2000), pp. 185–89.

149 Leonard M. Hammer, *A Foucauldian Approach to International Law: Descriptive Thoughts for Normative Issues* (Aldershot: Ashgate, 2007), p. 79.

150 Michel Foucault, 'Truth and Juridical Forms', in *Essential Works of Foucault, Vol. 3: Power*, pp. 1–89 (p. 4).

151 *Ibid.*, pp. 17–18.

152 *Ibid.*, p. 18.

153 *Ibid.*, p. 33.

154 *Ibid.*, p. 19.

155 *Ibid.*, p. 23.

156 *Ibid.*, p. 23.

157 *Ibid.*, p. 23.

158 *Ibid.*, p. 33.

159 *Ibid.*, p. 34.

160 *Ibid.*, p. 36.

161 *Ibid.*, p. 36.

162 *Ibid.*, p. 43.

163 *Ibid.*, p. 42.

164 *Ibid.*, p. 52.

165 *Ibid.*, p. 60.

166 *Ibid.*, p. 5.

167 *Ibid.*, p. 34.

168 *Ibid.*, p. 4.

169 *Ibid.*, p. 4.

170 Foucault, *Discipline and Punish*, p. 22.

171 *Ibid.*, p. 224.

172 Foucault, 'Truth and Juridical Forms', p. 4.

173 *Ibid.*, p. 4.0

Index